"Here is
a crys...
hold i...
the ...
drink it in; there is a hush
as we who have not seen
it before stand in a group
and watch it unfold."

Sir Alister Hardy
Great Waters, 1967

Aerial view of the southeast end of the island, looking northwest along the Salvesen Range with Drygalski Fjord and Hamilton Bay in the foreground.

Facing page Icebergs grounded between Annenkov Island and the mainland

A MESSAGE FROM HOWARD PEARCE

Welcome to South Georgia! I hope you enjoy your visit to one of the world's most pristine environments.

South Georgia's combination of spectacular scenery, outstanding wildlife and remoteness, together with its history of human endeavour, make it unique. This guide is designed to enhance your enjoyment of this very special place, and to enable you to help us preserve the Island in all its aspects for future generations.

My experience is that those who have been to South Georgia retain lasting memories of their visit and long to return. I hope that this will be your experience too. Until your return, the South Georgia website **www.sgisland.org** will help you to relive your memories, and provides an excellent means of keeping in touch with developments on the Island.

The South Georgia Government is committed to managing the Island in a responsible and sustainable way. If you have any suggestions which you think will help us with that task, please do not hesitate to let us know.

Howard J S Pearce

Howard J S Pearce CVO
Commissioner for South Georgia and
South Sandwich Islands

The Government of South Georgia and the South Sandwich Islands comprises of the Commissioner, Assistant Commissioner, Operations Manager, and Assistant Operations Manager. Based in the Falkland Islands, the Commissioner and Assistant Commissioner also hold the post of Governor and First Secretary, respectively, of the Falklands Islands Government, while the Operations team is employed full time on South Georgia issues. Working with the UK Foreign and Commonwealth Office these four people are responsible for the legal, financial and administrative governance of the island.

Left to right Richard McKee, Assistant Operations Manager; Harriet Hall, Assistant Commissioner; Howard Pearce, Commissioner; Gordon Liddle, Operations Manager (2005).

FOREWORD

Visitors to South Georgia can count themselves among the luckiest folk on earth. I know some who might disagree – but they will never know what they missed….

Islands by their very nature have always excited me. Some of the most irresistible are those upon which one may set foot, walk or scramble round their entire shoreline and be back at the landing point within the hour. It is easy to think "small" with islands. But South Georgia is something altogether different.

It is more like a "land" in its own right, with its own satellite islands, set there in the Southern Ocean, where an embracing sweep of the Antarctic Convergence proclaims it an "Antarctic" island in the true geographical as well as the climatic sense. Moreover, it looks it. The Allardyce Range has many a counterpart on the Antarctic Continent, but few are more impressive. Great tabular icebergs from the shelves of the far south thump along South Georgia's weather shore to become features of its beguiling landscape. There are sheltered valleys with meltwater streams, tussac grass covered moraines to offer a gentler echo of the Falklands, with close-up wildlife encounters to match. Visually, South Georgia has everything.

But there is an aura about this island that makes it not just special but unique. It is an aura born of history and human contact – humanity at times violent, callous and destructive – but with adventure and courage, endeavour and sacrifice uppermost.

A confirmed romantic, I cannot sit in the tussac by Cumberland Bay without trying to picture all those historic ships that dropped anchor in here on their way south – in the 'gateway to Antarctica'. Cook's *Resolution* passed this way in 1775, at the same time claiming the Island for Britain. Bellingshausen was here with *Vostok* and *Mirnyi* in 1819. At the turn of the century came Nordenskjöld in *Antarctic* and shortly afterwards, C. A. Larsen and the whalers. The scene was transformed then, with factories, steam and smoke and the clatter of machinery in the fjords and a sea red with the blood of whales.

One can picture exploration vessels running into hundreds; shades of Scott's *Discovery* and Shackleton's *Endurance* – and the little *Quest* aboard which he died in 1922, to be buried here in Grytviken, to leave a name now inseparable from the island.

Kim Crosbie and Sally Poncet have drawn on experts to detail some of these facets of South Georgia's past, its exciting present and offer predictions for the future. Here are all the facts on the rich animal and plant life, the geology and glaciology of the land and the oceanography of the surrounding sea.

Kim and Sally's "Visitor's Guide" is more than a robust little primer for a first visit, it is a testimony of their love for the place itself, a cry for the conservation of an irreplaceable island with a unique heritage for the world.

Then, when the visitors return home, this little book will become a treasured reminder of the good fortune that finally took them there – for years to come.

Keith Shackleton

Around The Shag Rocks Light-mantled Sooty Albatross
Oil; 30 × 48 inches; 1979; © Keith Shackleton RSMA, SWLA

CONTENTS

LIST OF FIGURES

LIST OF MAPS

ABOUT THIS GUIDE

Sally Poncet and Kim Crosbie

South Georgia is a mere speck in the immensity of the Southern Ocean, a 170 km long icy crescent, 2–40 km wide, and rising to 2,934 m. It covers 3,755 km² of which more than half is buried under permanent snow and ice. It has no trees, no permanent human population, and the closest inhabited land, the Falkland Islands, lies 1,400 km to the west, only slightly closer than Antarctica which is 1,500 km to the south.

For such a small island in such a remote and extreme part of the world, South Georgia generates an astounding depth of emotional attachment. Few visitors remain untouched by those unique qualities so warmly described by Keith Shackleton in his foreword, and the small international community of people who are closely involved with the island possess not only a solid core of factual knowledge but also a very caring concern for the island and its future. The first section of this guide presents a range of specialist contributions

from a number of these people, each with expert knowledge of the topics covered. The second section contains detailed descriptions of 24 of South Georgia's most popular visitor sites. Then, drawing on our collective experience and knowledge of the island amassed over the past twenty five years, we present information about each site's history, wildlife, landing beaches and hikes, accompanied by photographs and large-scale maps.

The information shown on these maps includes the location of wildlife, vegetation, historic artefacts and topographical features of interest. The 'features' column for each site provides a summary of that information.

Tips on how to avoid disturbing the wildlife and environment when visiting the sites are listed in the 'pointers' column. Some of South Georgia's special features are highlighted in a series of 'boxes' interspersed throughout the book.
They contain information on a diverse range of topics including key wildlife species, populations in decline, introduced species, and life at a whaling station. There is a checklist of South Georgia's wildlife and plant species, a wildlife calendar showing the breeding cycles of the island's birds, some contact addresses and suggestions for further reading.

TIPS FOR VISITORS

Some local facts

South Georgia is a United Kingdom Overseas Territory, administered by the Government of South Georgia and the South Sandwich Islands through the Office of the Commissioner in Stanley, Falkland Islands. Sovereignty of the island is also claimed by Argentina. English is currently the official language and the local currency is the Falkland Islands pound, although British sterling, Euros and American dollars are accepted at the South Georgia Museum and local post office. The island's official time zone is Greenwich Mean Time −2 hours.

Obtaining a visitor permit

All visitors require a Visitor Permit before arriving at the island. This is obtained by applying to the Commissioner. Application forms and supporting documents are available from the office of the Commissioner in Stanley (see page 174) and are also available on-line at the website **www.sgisland.org**. Cruise ship and charter yacht operators usually complete applications on behalf of their clients. Once the application requirements are met, visitors are issued with a Visitor Permit which is presented by the Government Officer at King Edward Point on arrival of the vessel and after payment of a landing fee.

All visitors are required to abide by the provisions in the document *Information for Visitors to South Georgia*, which is issued with the application form. Only cruise ship operators that are members of the International Association of Antarctica Tour Operators (IAATO) are allowed to land at sites other than Grytviken, but with the provision that they carry guides who have sub-Antarctic or equivalent experience in remote areas.

Where you may go

In total there are over 40 sites around the island which are visited by tourists. Each Visitor Permit application must list all sites which are intended to be visited. Certain areas that are rat-free and vulnerable to disturbance are protected by stringent rules. Some places (e.g. Bird, Cooper and Annenkov Islands) are closed to tourism altogether. At others, namely Prion Island, Cape Rosa and Larsen Harbour, special codes of conduct apply to prevent the accidental introduction of rats and to minimise trampling nest sites of South Georgia pipits and burrowing seabirds.

With the exception of Grytviken, all the whaling stations are now closed to visitors. They are in a dangerous state of disrepair, and hazardous materials such as windblown corrugated iron and asbestos particles are of particular concern. Conspicuous signs on the outskirts of the stations advise visitors not to enter or approach within 200 m. Wherever you visit, please remember it is not permitted to remove any plants, animals or historical artefacts.

Viewing wildlife

Wildlife protection at South Georgia is based on the principle that visitors give wildlife right-of-way at all

times. While an animal may choose to come closer, visitors must back off if their presence looks likely to cause changes in the animal's behaviour. As a general guide, approach distances that may help minimise disturbance are 5–10 m from all breeding birds and elephant seals, 10 m from all nesting albatross species and moulting birds, 25 m from displaying wandering albatrosses, and at least 15 m from fur seals. The wildlife protection guidelines in the *Information for Visitors to South Georgia* document contain more details on how to minimise disturbance. Take note of these and of the special code of conduct for visitors to Prion Island.

Light-induced seabird strikes

Seabirds are often attracted to ships' lights, particularly on misty nights. The birds become disorientated by the lights and may be injured or killed on collision with the vessel. The species most commonly affected are Antarctic prions, blue petrels, diving petrels and storm-petrels. Employing some simple mitigation measures, both when the ship is at anchor and underway, can help minimize bird strikes. Deck lighting and ice-lights should be kept to a minimum level for safe operations when navigating in South Georgia waters and while at anchor, particularly on nights when visibility is poor and when in the vicinity of seabird colonies. Black-out blinds should be used on all portholes and windows. Birds found on deck should be handled as little as possible. Keep them in a warm dark room until ready for release. Ideally each bird should be kept in a separate container but if boxes are in short supply, keep each species separate and only a few birds in each box to avoid suffocation. Release when the deck lighting is off or at first light next day – and after first making sure there are no skuas around!

For your safety

Ensuring that you are adequately clothed and equipped for severe and changeable weather and sea conditions is an important part of personal safety, as is being alert to the movement of wildlife around you. In certain coastal areas where fur seals throng the beaches and adjacent tussac areas, extra vigilance is required, especially during the main breeding season (mid-November to mid-January) when the seals are aggressively territorial. Fur seals can move faster than you can run, and they have a particularly nasty bite that is prone to infection. For your own safety and to avoid unnecessary disturbance to the seals, it is usually preferable to avoid landing on these beaches during their breeding season.

The thinning of the ozone layer in the Antarctic also affects South Georgia, particularly in October and November when the risk of sunburn is at its highest. Wearing a hat, high factor sun cream and sunglasses even on a cloudy day and always when out on the water or snow are standard precautions.

When hiking, avoid venturing on to glaciers without specialist equipment or ice experience, as most of the ice fields are heavily crevassed and unsurveyed. When referring to the 1958 DOS topographic map of the island, be aware that many landmark features – glaciers and shorelines in particular – have changed beyond recognition due to the significant retreat and thinning of the island's cover of ice and permanent snowfields. These changes are readily apparent when comparing the 1958 map with the most recent topographic map, BAS (Misc) 12A, 2004.

Field huts located at St. Andrews Bay, Maiviken, Lyell Glacier, Greene Peninsula, Corral Bay, Jason Harbour and Sorling Beach are still used intermittently by scientific parties and expeditions. Any equipment or food they contain is for emergency use only. Be sure to close the door securely on leaving.

Fresh water at South Georgia is reputedly the best in the world – unless it's flowed through a penguin or seal colony first, so make sure that your drinking water comes direct from glacier and snowfield meltwater streams.

When hiking in the vicinity of Grytviken, be aware of unexploded ordnance dating from the 1982 conflict and subsequent military presence. Treat any suspect objects with caution. Do not touch them, but note their position, place a marker nearby and inform the Government Officer immediately with a description of size, shape, colour, markings, condition and quantity.

Going ashore

Regardless of how long you think you might be spending ashore, be prepared for a wide range of weather conditions and take adequate clothing and a minimum of survival equipment to allow you to wait out a 'blow' on shore should this situation ever arise. Even on calm sunny days, keep an eye on the mountaintops for spindrift (windblown snow and ice crystals), which is often the first indicator of a strong wind approaching. South Georgia's weather changes constantly with the ceaseless passage of Southern Ocean weather systems coming in from the west, and sudden changes in weather are the rule rather than the exception.

Temperatures in the summer months are usually between 0°C and +10°C, although on windless, cloudless days or when a föhn wind is blowing, temperatures have been known to rise to over +20°C. Equally, summer snow squalls and blizzard conditions may send temperatures plummeting to the equivalent of -20°C due to the wind chill effect.

The most practical clothes to wear ashore are medium-weight layers of thermal garments with waterproof boots, jacket and trousers. Outer clothing made of a breathable fabric is preferable when hiking.

For landings on surf-washed beaches and hikes on boggy inland valleys and muddy coastal slopes, a pair of knee-high rubber boots with sturdy, high-traction soles are invaluable. Another useful piece of equipment is a collapsible hiking pole or walking stick for scrambling up and down tussac slopes and over rough terrain.

Be sure to protect your equipment adequately when going ashore. There will probably be at least one occasion when you will be rain- and spray-drenched, or blasted by particles of wind-borne sand or grit, so it makes sense to carry fragile items in drybags or heavy-duty, self-sealing plastic bags. They are a must for landings, regardless of how fine the weather – in a matter of minutes, the surf could be up and a 40 knot wind blowing. A sturdy waterproof case provides the ultimate protection. Arm yourself with these items plus a couple of pairs of gloves, a warm hat and binoculars and a backpack (not forgetting the sunscreen and sunglasses) and you are ready for a landing. Once ashore, take care not to inadvertently drop batteries and film canisters, and hang on tightly to plastic bags and lens papers or a sudden gust may whisk them away to litter the landscape and entangle wildlife.

Photography

For all photography, be it using video, digital or traditional photographic equipment, and regardless of whether the shots are for personal or professional use, the first rule of thumb is to avoid disturbing wildlife. Approach any bird or animal subject slowly, and keep to the recommended wildlife approach distances. Be aware of surrounding wildlife and try to avoid causing any changes in their behaviour. Some of your best photos could be those you take while sitting on the beach where patience will be rewarded by close encounters with curious penguins and seals that gather in small groups to inspect any newcomers.

Cold temperatures reduce battery life so carry extra batteries in a warm inner pocket to increase their efficiency. Zoom lenses eliminate the need for frequent changing of lenses and exposing the front of your camera to the elements. They also enable the taking of close-up pictures of wildlife without unnecessary extra movement or approaching animals too closely. If there is any sign of disturbance from wildlife, regardless of your distance from it, back off. Photography is not over when the shutter clicks; it is important to retreat slowly from the subject in the same way that it was approached.

Think about other people too when taking photos, particularly those who simply want to enjoy the scenery and wildlife with their own eyes instead of through the lens of a camera. Respect their choice and give them the same space and privacy you give the wildlife. In fact, we encourage every photographer to put cameras to one side every now and then, and take the time to just sit a while and fully absorb the wilderness and beauty of the South Georgia landscape.

Left (top to bottom) Fields of bergy bits and brash; zodiac approaching macaroni penguin colony; watching king penguins; visitors at Gold Harbour king penguin colony

OCEANS AND CLIMATE

Mark Brandon,
The Open University

South Georgia lies in the path of the Antarctic Circumpolar Current (ACC) which flows continuously in an easterly direction around Antarctica between about latitudes 50° and 60° south. The ACC effectively isolates the Antarctic continent from the warmer waters to the north, and, over the course of time, it was partially responsible for the formation of Antarctica's permanent ice cover. Although driven by the strong prevailing westerly winds, the path of the current is also determined by the topography of the sea floor. On entering the Scotia Sea through the narrow neck of Drake Passage, the current encounters the extensive trough and canyon ridge system that connects South America to the Antarctic Peninsula. South Georgia lies right in the centre of its path, and the island is thus effectively surrounded entirely by cold Antarctic water of fairly uniform salinity and temperature between 2°C and 4°C in the summer and 0°C and -1°C in the winter.

The northern and southern boundaries (or ocean fronts) of the ACC are well defined by marked differences in temperature. The northern boundary is called the Polar Front (formerly the Antarctic Convergence). It lies about 350 km north of South Georgia although its exact position is affected by local meanders and eddies. On any voyage between the Falklands and South Georgia, the passage across the Polar Front is marked by a rapid drop in the sea surface temperature – as much as 2°C within half a degree of latitude – with a total fall from around 6°C to 2°C. The temperature change is often associated with mist which forms as warm air meets cold water. At the southern boundary of the ACC,

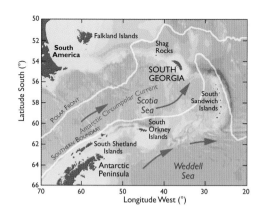

temperatures change again, falling from around 2°C to between +1°C and -1·5°C.

Sea ice rarely forms at South Georgia except in sheltered fjords in the winter and, although pack ice has been recorded up to 200 km northeast of the island in the past, the ice edge usually lies well to the south. Numerous icebergs carried by the ACC frequently drift past the island, generated both locally from calving glaciers and from the disintegration of large Antarctic ice shelves, and in 2004, several large icebergs, each over half the length of the island, grounded on the edge of the continental shelf about 40 km offshore, causing major problems for shipping as they disintegrated into a myriad of tabular bergs, bergy bits and brash ice.

Being such a small island, it is no surprise that the ocean and the ACC in particular exert a major influence on South Georgia's regional climate. The magnitude of this influence is apparent when you consider that although South Georgia is approximately the same distance from the South Pole as southern England is from the North Pole, over half of South Georgia is covered in permanent ice, whilst Britain has none. Equally, the island's permanent snow line is about 300-400 m above sea level, while at this altitude, the coastline of the Beagle Channel area in Tierra del Fuego (virtually the same latitude but on the north side of the ACC), is covered in trees.

The cooling effect of the ocean on the ambient air temperature is a key factor contributing to the island's typically cold, wet and windy, maritime climate. Ocean-borne moisture-laden air coming in from the west nourishes the large snow and ice fields that cover over half the island. Winter and summer seasons are clearly defined. Snow can mantle the entire island from May to October, and the average annual winter temperature at sea level is 0°C to –1°C, with –19°C being the lowest recorded. In summer, temperatures at sea level average between 3°C and 5°C. The effects of global warming on mean annual and seasonal temperatures are noticeable, with an overall rise in temperature of +0·6°C in the past century.

The other main factor driving local climate is the interaction between the prevailing westerly winds and the island's 2,000-3,000 m high mountain ranges. This gigantic backbone of rock and ice runs the entire length of the island, creating marked regional climatic differences between the central northeast coast and the island's extremities and exposed southwest coast. The latter in particular is cooler, damper and more extensively glaciated than the central northeast coast. Lying in the lee of the Allardyce Range and

protected by the massive ramparts of Mount Paget, the Cumberland and Stromness Bay areas in particular enjoy distinctly warmer, sunnier and drier weather than the rest of the island – and on certain cloudless, windless summer days, the visitor might well wonder if the island's reputation for Antarctic-style weather is a myth.

The most striking feature of the island's climate however, is the rapidity with which conditions may change: föhn winds (formed when air masses are forced to rise over the mountain ranges, and then descend the lee slopes in dry, warm and violent gusts) can raise temperatures by over 10°C within 10 minutes; and a blizzard and sub-zero temperatures can appear out of nowhere on a calm sunny afternoon. Regular phenomena are the violent gusts of wind known as williwaws that are funnelled down the glaciated valleys and tear across the bays like mini-tornadoes at 100 knots or more. Without a doubt, it is the weather that dominates the South Georgia landscape for visitors and wildlife alike.

Monthly mean max/min temperatures (*above*), rainfall and cloud cover (*below*) at Grytviken, South Georgia 1971-1995.

GEOLOGY

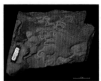

Fossil trail left by unknown marine bivalve found in Royal Bay.

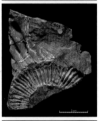

Fossil impression of ammonite found on Annenkov Island

Fossil impression of bivalve found on Annenkov Island

Phil Stone,
British Geological
Survey

South Georgia provides some of the most breath-taking scenery in the Southern Ocean. Snow and ice-covered peaks stand stark and beautiful, continually battered by the storms that sweep eastwards across the island. The Allardyce Range runs like a spine down the length of the island, and rises to 2,934 m on the summit of Mt. Paget. In the southeast of the island the mountains form the Salvesen Range whose highest peak is Mount Carse at 2,330 m. But why do these mountains rise more or less straight from the sea with no other land for hundreds of miles in any direction?

This rocky outpost in the South Atlantic owes its existence to the massive tectonic forces that inexorably drive huge crustal plates across the surface of the globe. As the Atlantic Ocean has opened over the last 200 million years, the South American Plate has over-ridden the Pacific Plate with the join running down the coast of Chile. The Pacific Ocean crust dives down beneath South America (a process called subduction) but south of Tierra del Fuego something different happens. There, the Scotia Sea forms a great wedge eastwards into the Atlantic as far as the South Sandwich Islands. Beneath those islands the subduction direction is reversed, with the Atlantic Ocean crust diving down under the Scotia Sea to produce that archipelago's active volcanoes. Whilst the spreading Atlantic Ocean has been destroyed by subduction at this South Sandwich "join", elsewhere the Atlantic has kept growing, driving South America ever westwards over the Pacific and further from the South Sandwich Islands. So, over tens of millions of years,

a huge fracture zone has formed along the northern side of the Scotia Sea, within which fragments of southern South America have been broken off and abandoned. One such piece of continental jetsam is now South Georgia.

The story began before the Atlantic Ocean existed, when Africa and South America formed part of a vast, continuous landmass called Gondwana. The granites and gneisses (*Drygalski Fjord Complex*) that form the Salvesen Range date from that era and are the oldest rocks on the island. They originated along the margin of Gondwana, but by 150 million years ago had split away to provide a foundation for a chain of volcanoes. Between the volcanoes and the remains of Gondwana lay an expanding marine basin in which lavas were erupted (*Larsen Harbour Formation*) and volcanic ash accumulated (*Annenkov Island Formation*). By 130 million years ago, sediment eroded from the opposing sides of the basin was being deposited as new sandstone and mudstone layers with contrasting compositions: the *Cumberland Bay Formation* came from the volcanic side whilst the *Sandebugten Formation* came from the continental, Gondwana, side.

About 90 million years ago, a major shift in the direction of plate movement destroyed the basin. The rocks on the volcanic side of the basin were driven up and over those on the continental side, and the different types and ages of rock were jumbled together. Finally, South Georgia was torn away from South America, then abandoned 2,000 km to the east of Cape Horn during the formation of the Scotia Arc.

Most of today's landscape is made up of myriad layers of sandstone and mudstone, of which the volcaniclastic sediments of the *Cumberland Bay Formation* are the most widespread. They extend from the extreme northwest of the island southeast to Iris Bay, whilst the quartzose, continental sediments of the *Sandebugten Formation* underlie the area between Barff Peninsula and Gold Harbour. The individual sediment layers of both these formations are up to 2 m thick and continuous for many kilometres. They were formed from huge submarine flows of chaotically mixed sediment called "turbidity currents". The flows accelerated down the sides of the basin but slowed abruptly as they spread out across its floor. As they slowed, their sediment load settled out; first, the largest and heaviest particles, then, progressively, smaller and lighter grains. The result is a "graded bed" with coarse sand at its base and sequentially finer sand and silt appearing towards the top; between successive turbidity flows only mud was deposited. This alternation produces the striped appearance of many Allardyce Range crags.

Fossils are quite rare, with most occurring in the *Annenkov Island Formation*. There, shell impressions illustrate the kind of bivalve shellfish that lived on the seabed, whilst various kinds of ammonite and belemnite fossils are the remains of invertebrates that swam above them. More common, and found throughout the sedimentary rocks of South Georgia, are the traces left behind by soft-bodied animals as they foraged through the sand and mud. Their tracks and trails have been widely preserved in the ensuing sandstone and mudstone.

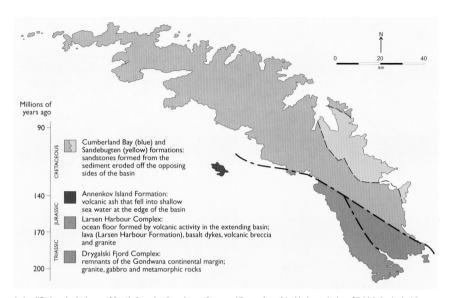

Millions of years ago

CRETACEOUS
90

JURASSIC
140
170

TRIASSIC
200

Cumberland Bay (blue) and Sandebugten (yellow) formations: sandstones formed from the sediment eroded off the opposing sides of the basin

Annenkov Island Formation: volcanic ash that fell into shallow sea water at the edge of the basin

Larsen Harbour Complex: ocean floor formed by volcanic activity in the extending basin; lava (Larsen Harbour Formation), basalt dykes, volcanic breccia and granite

Drygalski Fjord Complex: remnants of the Gondwana continental margin; granite, gabbro and metamorphic rocks

A simplified geological map of South Georgia. Based upon Stone and Tanner (2004) by kind permission of British Geological Survey.

The alternating layers of sandstone and mudstone in the Cumberland Bay Formation give many rock faces in the Allardyce Range a strongly striped appearance.

Alternating layers of sandstone and mudstone from the Cumberland Bay Formation at Prince Olav Harbour.

GLACIERS AND LANDFORMS

Over the last few million years, ice caps and glaciers have sculpted the remarkable scenery of South Georgia. The extent of the ice has fluctuated over time and today just over 50% of the island is covered in permanent snow and ice. The south coast is more extensively glaciated than the north coast, reflecting the high snowfall on the windward side of the island. Here, heavily crevassed glaciers descend steeply from the mountains to the coast. On the more indented north coast, large glaciers terminate in wide, calving icefronts in the fjords, and the intervening peninsulas form the largest expanses of ice-free ground on the island. The permanent snowline rises from about 300 metres above sea level on the south coast to about 450 to 600 metres above sea level on the north coast.

In the past, during the coldest parts of the Ice Age, an ice cap covered all the low ground and extended offshore to the edge of the continental shelf around the island; only the higher summits stood above the surface of the ice. During warmer periods, like that of the present day, the ice cover has been more restricted. Following the last glacial maximum, about 22,000 years ago, the glaciers retreated within the fjords where they halted or advanced sometime before 10,000 years ago, forming well-defined moraine ridges. The glaciers then retreated further, inside their present limits, but advanced again around 2,000 years ago, and also during the late 19th century. Since then, they have generally been retreating, although they re-advanced briefly between 1925 and 1935.

John Gordon,
Scottish Natural
Heritage

The fronts of many glaciers have retreated markedly within the last few decades, creating inlets, lagoons and beaches where none existed previously. At Gold Harbour, the lower section of Bertrab Glacier has disappeared entirely, exposing a large rock step which 30 years ago was covered by a spectacular icefall. Some small corrie glaciers have shrunk drastically and are now close to disappearing (e.g. Hodges Glacier, near Grytviken). These changes are related to climate warming, particularly since about 1950. Interestingly, however, they have not affected all of South Georgia's glaciers equally; some of the largest tidewater glaciers have changed comparatively little over the past few decades and one of the largest, Novosilski Glacier on the south coast, has actually advanced. The behaviour of these calving glaciers is more complicated because they are partly floating, but if the climate warming continues, then they too may retreat dramatically.

The landscape of South Georgia displays many classic glacial landforms. These include impressive glacial troughs and fjords with characteristic truncated spurs and over-deepened rock basins, as well as many corries along the flanks of the mountains. The glaciers have also scoured and roughened the lower ground, forming rocky knolls and small lake basins. Along the sides of the valleys and fjords, end and lateral moraines record the former positions of the glaciers. A particularly fine example can be seen on the approach to Grytviken: Moraine Fjord, which is nearly 200 metres deep, is all but closed off by the terminal moraine reef that stretches across its mouth. Meltwater rivers emerging from the retreating land-based glaciers have formed gravelly outwash plains with braided channels inland from the coast (e.g. Salisbury Plain in the Bay of Isles).

Raised beaches occur as clearly visible, tussac-covered terraces inland from the modern beaches at altitudes of about 3m and 7m above present sea level. An indirect effect of glaciation, they result from isostatic rebound of the land following earlier glacier retreat. Good examples occur at King Edward Point and elsewhere on the north coast where they provided flat land for the construction of the former whaling stations.

In ice-free areas, the effects of frost action in the soil are often clearly displayed as patterned ground, including sorted stone stripes and sorted circles, and in widespread solifluction lobes formed by the seasonal creep of the soil downslope.

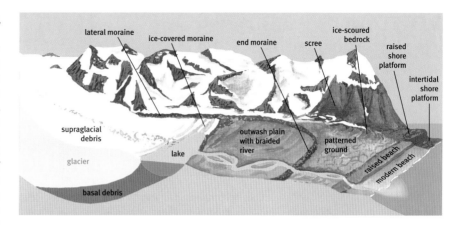

The centre black strips of medial moraine indicate where glaciers have joined together

21

VEGETATION

South Georgia has 25 native species of vascular plants, over 50 naturalised introduced vascular species (found mostly around the old whaling stations) and about 125 species of mosses, 85 of liverworts and 200 of lichens. There are no known endemic vascular plant species, although there are a few endemic mosses and lichens. The vegetation is similar to that on other sub-Antarctic islands, lush but low-growing, and with the usual absence of shrubs and trees. See to the plant checklist on page 168.

During the summer months, the lower snow- and ice-free areas, with their mix of scree slopes, rocky bluffs, gravel moraines and vegetation, appear as a mosaic of browns and greens, in striking contrast to the ice-capped mountains above. The site maps in this guide show the three most common vegetation communities on the island. These are tussac grassland, *Festuca* grassland and fellfield. In addition, scattered throughout are smaller areas of bog, mire and herbfield communities. Although defined and mapped as distinct communities, they effectively intergrade imperceptibly with each other so that clear-cut boundaries are uncommon.

The plant species in these communities have had to master the art of living in an extreme environment, each one adapting to a range of environmental factors – shelter, aspect, nutrients, water, snow, grazing and trampling by animals – all of which determine their distribution. For example, tussac grassland, dominated by the large tussock-forming grass *Parodiochloa flabellata*, forms a conspicuous green coastal fringe around the entire island.

This tussac is particularly luxuriant and a darker shade of green where there is nitrogen enrichment from birds and seals. Depending on topography and aspect and hence the degree of shelter, tussac grassland may extend inland up to 200–300 m altitude.

In contrast, *Festuca* grassland occurs mainly along the relatively sheltered central part of the north coast from Fortuna Bay to Gold Harbour. It is dominated by *Festuca contracta*, a light-brown to yellow grass common on lower to mid-altitude slopes above the coastal tussac fringe. Where the ground is wet underfoot, *Festuca* grassland merges into areas of bog and mire made up of dark-brown expanses of the rush *Rostkovia magellanica*, scattered patches of bright-green and russet mosses, and light-green swards of Antarctic hairgrass *Deschampsia antarctica* mixed with the rush *Juncus scheuchzerioides*.

Patches of the short woody-stemmed burnet *Acaena magellanica* are locally common in a range of communities, often intermixing with other small herbs, mosses and lichens. Where it forms continuous stands, the blue-green hue of this herbfield community creates subtle colour contrasts amongst the tussac and *Festuca* grasslands. On the central north coast it is heavily grazed by reindeer, which have transformed former herbfield communities into *Festuca* grasslands over much of their foraging range.

Jenny Scott,
University of
Tasmania

At higher altitudes above the climatic limit of tussac and *Festuca* grasslands, the vegetation consists of a sparse scattering of grasses, small herbs, mosses and lichens growing on predominantly bare ground. Known as fellfield, this community is also found at sea level on moraines and moraine outwash areas adjacent to glaciers where it often represents the initial stages of vegetation development on recently deglaciated land.

Plant communities on the south coast of the island – where climatic conditions are harsher – and also on the offshore islands, are dominated by tussac grassland on the lower coastal areas and by fellfield on the higher rock and scree slopes, where mosses, lichens, Antarctic hairgrass and herbfield are common.

Top (left to right) Tussac in flower; shield fern; red flower-head of the native burnet.
Bottom Lowland fellfield in Shackleton Valley (*left*) and the distinctive yellow-brown of *Festuca* grasslands in the foreground with green swathes of tussac grassland behind (*right*).
Facing page (*right*) Antarctic buttercup

WILDLIFE

Fur seal breeding beach at Prince Olav Harbour during the height of the breeding season

The sheer abundance of seals, penguins and petrels that gather annually in huge concentrations along South Georgia's coastal fringe makes the island one of the most remarkable wildlife spectacles on Earth. That, and the trusting manner in which visitors are surrounded by wildlife, create unforgettable visual and emotional memories.

The animals return each year principally to breed, but also to moult or to rest between foraging trips at sea. A summary of the year's breeding events is shown in the wildlife calendar (page 171). Evolutionary forces have created the necessary physiological adaptations that allow each species to transit seamlessly between two strikingly different environments: the vast expanses of the circumpolar ocean and its relatively stable, food-laden environment, and the tiny speck of rocky shoreline, where there is no food, where temperatures fluctuate widely and space is at a premium on the narrow strip of shoreline.

On stepping ashore, visitors are often overwhelmed by the huge numbers of animals gathered on the beaches; a teeming mosaic of colour and sound as half a million king penguins, 400,000 elephant seals and several million fur seals jostle for breeding territories. Look closer and other species become evident: skuas, sheathbills and giant petrels dart in amongst the penguins and seals, the new-born, the dead and the dying, as they scavenge for eggs, chicks, and seal placenta. South Georgia pintails feed in the intertidal zone at the water's edge or scurry to the shelter of the tussac. This small brown duck has even been known to indulge in the odd meal of carrion, and it is common at most sites around the island with

its distinctive low-pitched whistle providing a discreet evocative call amid the roar of surf and seals. Less abundant is its cousin, the speckled teal, which is mostly seen in the Grytviken area.

Macaroni, chinstrap, gentoo and king penguins return each year to breed in the same area, either on the beach itself or in the tussac grassland adjacent. Tussac grass is the most important wildlife habitat on the island (see tussac diagram on page 83) and is used extensively by seals and seabirds for breeding, resting and moulting. It may vary considerably in appearance, ranging from dark to mid-green, sometimes yellowish-green, depending on the nutrient status of the soil – generally, the heavier the degree of fertilising from seal or seabird concentrations, the darker the tussac.

On the rat-free areas of the south coast and offshore islands, these areas of dark green tussac also indicate colonies of small burrowing seabirds such as Antarctic prions, blue petrels, and both species of diving petrels which have been all but eliminated by rats along the north coast of mainland South Georgia. These petrels are also hunted by the brown skua. Efficient predators, skuas pick each carcass clean, often leaving only a pair of wings as evidence of the slaughter. The South Georgia pipit – an endemic species and the only passerine found on the island – is also confined to these rat-free areas, although a few are occasionally seen at Cooper Bay, stragglers from nearby Cooper Island.

Many of South Georgia's seabirds are cliff-nesting. Cape petrels, snow petrels and blue-eyed shags breed on cliff ledges and rock outcrops at numerous localities around the island. In contrast

SOUTH GEORGIA WILDLIFE HABITATS

KEY

① Snow petrels on cliff ledges

② Wilson's storm-petrels in boulder scree

③ Black-browed and grey-headed albatrosses on steep coastal tussac

④ Fur seals in dark green tussac

⑤ Fur seal breeding beach

⑥ Light-mantled sooty albatrosses on cliffs

⑦ Cape petrels on cliff ledges

⑧ Antarctic terns on outwash plain

⑨ South Georgia diving petrels in scree

⑩ Gentoo penguin colony

⑪ King penguin colony + elephant seal breeding beach

⑫ Macaroni penguin colony + snowy sheathbill

⑬ Brown skua nest

⑭ South Georgia pintails

⑮ Northern + southern giant petrels

⑯ Wandering albatrosses

⑰ Blue-eyed shag colony

⑱ Common diving petrels in steep tussac

⑲ White-chinned petrels

⑳ Antarctic prions

㉑ South Georgia pipits in rat-free areas

㉒ Blue petrels on north-facing tussac slopes

㉓ Kelp gulls

Four of South Georgia's resident penguin species
From left to right – king, macaroni, gentoo and chinstrap

Elephant and fur seals haul out near three trypots at Elsehul

black-browed and grey-headed albatrosses nest in large colonies on steep coastal slopes and cliffs on the mainland and several offshore islands. There are around 75,000 black-browed albatross pairs breeding at approximately 20 sites from Willis Islands to Clerke Rocks off the east end of South Georgia. Grey-heads, of which there are nearly 48,000 pairs, are concentrated at eight locations at the northwest extremity, often in association with black-brows. Light-mantled sooty albatrosses are less gregarious, nesting in small scattered groups or sometimes singly on steep tussac slopes and coastal cliffs along virtually all of South Georgia's coastline.

Wandering albatrosses prefer gently undulating tussac grasslands and are found at 30 sites around the island. Since 1984, their total population is estimated to have declined by 30%, and there are now only about 1,550 pairs nesting each year, of which over 60% are on Bird Island.

Walking inland to the fellfield areas and beyond, where glaciers, rock faces, scree slopes dominate the landscape, the absence of wildlife contrasts sharply with the crowed beaches below. However, these regions are not entirely destitute of life: the observant hiker may spot snow petrels circling the snow-covered peaks above, while underfoot in the scree and boulder fields, are Wilson's storm-petrels, South Georgia diving petrels and Antarctic prions. These petrels nest underground in burrows and rock crevices, safe from the predatory rats that are restricted to the shelter of coastal tussac.

Left (top to bottom) Wandering albatross; black-browed albatross; grey-headed albatross; light-mantled sooty albatross.
Right Perimylopid beetle

Antarctic terns also breed in these rocky wastes, their eggs and chicks well camouflaged in the rocky scrapes that serve as nests. Being out in the open, the parents have ample warning of approaching danger, and at the sight of a distant intruder, band together in pairs or small groups, chattering angrily and swooping down on the unsuspecting walker.

In this way, different species make use of different habitats to survive: the beach with its easy access to the sea; the shelter of dense tussac and underground burrows; coastal cliffs; inland scree slopes and mountain ledges. For more information about seals, see pages 116 and 156.

Terrestial fauna

In comparison with insect populations on other sub-Antarctic islands the diversity and number of South Georgia's invertebrates is relatively low due to the island's severe climatic conditions. Nonetheless, invertebrates are the most abundant native terrestrial fauna on the island. To date there have been nine species of beetle recorded (including one freshwater diving beetle and an alien species introduced from the Falklands), 14 species of flies (Diptera), four of spiders, one earthworm species, over 60 of mites and numerous springtails. Relatively inconspicuous, most species occupy specific niches along the habitat gradient that ranges from the shoreline up to about 600 m above sea level.

INTRODUCED SPECIES

The rich diversity and astounding abundance of South Georgia's wildlife set amid the island's magnificent scenery give visitors a memorable impression of unspoilt wilderness. However, most of the areas visited have in fact been markedly modified by people and by the animals and plants they brought with them, either intentionally or accidentally. A prime example is that of the Norwegian whalers who unwittingly introduced dandelions to the island by following the custom of including a handful of native Norwegian soil in the graves of their dead. Today, large stands of dandelions can be found near the Husvik, Grytviken and Leith Harbour cemeteries. Pristine wilderness areas still exist on offshore islands, the remote south coast and inland mountain regions. Elsewhere, the landscape is slowly being altered by introduced mammals, plants and insects that thrive alongside the teeming penguin colonies and fur seal beaches.

Introductions of non-native animals and plants started in the late 1700s when the first sealers arrived at the island, bringing with them Norway rats, house mice and annual meadow-grass. Like all Southern Ocean islands, South Georgia's native wildlife has evolved in the absence of any land mammals, and the introduction of some alien species - in particular rats and reindeer - has had devastating effects on the island's ecosystem.

Norway rats are widespread and abundant along virtually the entire length of South Georgia's northern coastline. They are not found on the harsher more exposed south coast areas between Drygalski Fjord and King Haakon Bay or on most offshore islands. Here, the barriers of sea, glaciers and potentially climate have so far proved effective in limiting their range. However the risk of rats spreading to these areas is ever-present, either through accidental introductions by people, or as glaciers continue to retreat and temperatures rise.

The impact of rats on the island's birds has been immeasurable. They feed on eggs and chicks and prey on adult South Georgia pipits and small burrowing petrels. These species are now confined almost exclusively to rat-free offshore islands and the rat-free mainland areas of the south coast. The larger white-chinned petrels and the South Georgia pintail still survive in rat-infested areas, despite eggs and young chicks being taken.

As well as the accidental arrivals, a variety of animals - sheep, goats, pigs, cattle, reindeer, rabbits, poultry, pigeons, dogs and cats - were introduced at various times to provide food for expeditions and the whaling stations. With the exception of reindeer, none have survived in the wild.

From approximately 20 reindeer introduced from Norway between 1911 and 1925, there is now a thriving population of over 3,000 animals split into two herds that occupy the central north coast area of the island. Separated by glaciers, the southern herd grazes the entire coastline from Barff Peninsula south to the northern shore of Royal Bay, while the smaller northern herd is confined to the

PREVENTING THE SPREAD OF RATS AND MICE

All rat-free areas have been proposed as Environmentally Sensitive Areas, one of several measures aimed at minimising the risk of accidental rodent introductions. The most frequently visited rat-free areas are Bird Island, Larsen Harbour, and Cape Rosa at the entrance to King Haakon Bay, and Albatross and Prion Islands in the Bay of Isles. Visitors to these sites, and particularly those who are camping or travelling round the island from rat-infested to rat-free areas, must take every precaution to keep rats and mice out of those areas that are rodent-free.

- Place all foodstuffs and, as far as possible, other equipment, in robust containers which are secured in such a manner so that any rodent entry would be readily apparent.
- Make sure the packing facility is rodent-free before filling containers.
- Do not leave boxes open overnight during packing.
- Immediately before loading, carefully re-inspect the cargo for animal signs in unsealed containers.
- Carry out further checks for signs of rodents while unloading is in progress on to the landing boat and when the cargo is landed ashore, and ensure that the landing boat is free of rodents.
- When moored alongside a jetty, ensure that no foodstuffs are left on deck and that hatches are secure, particularly at night when rats are most likely to come on board.
- Use rat-guards when moored alongside jetties, both in South Georgia and any ports visited before arrival at the island.

area between Fortuna Bay and the northern shores of Cumberland West Bay.

Throughout their range, reindeer have drastically altered the vegetation by over-grazing the native grasses and in particular tussac, as well as certain lichens and the native burnet. They are also contributing to the spread of the introduced annual meadow-grass, and their well-trodden tracks have become a conspicuous feature of the landscape. Favourite grazing areas are often close to gentoo penguin colonies, where the 'greens' of annual meadow-grass flourish particularly well due to an ample supply of nutrients provided by the birds. Some good examples of lush 'greens' are those at Whistle Cove in Fortuna Bay, on the north-facing slopes of Godthul and in Olsen Valley near Husvik.

In 2002 and 2003, small numbers of reindeer were shipped to the Falklands, and there are plans to eradicate at least one of the two herds.

Left Flies feeding on flowers of the introduced dandelion
Facing page Members of the 1955-56 South Georgia Survey establishing a camp site

THE DISCOVERY OF SOUTH GEORGIA

Robert Burton,
South Georgia
Association

During the 17th and 18th centuries, ships making the perilous rounding of Cape Horn were sometimes swept off course by storms. Survival rather than exploration was the priority, but there were occasional reports of land. The first documented sighting of South Georgia was from a London merchant Antoine de la Roché in April 1675. The 350 ton vessel on which he was a passenger was blown off course while returning to Europe from Peru, and although the original records of the voyage and the name of the ship have been lost, an account written by a Spanish captain indicates that the ship spent two weeks sheltering in a large bay – possibly Drygalski Fjord – in sight of '*Snow Mountains*'.

The next sighting was reported in 1756 by French merchants on board the Spanish ship *Léon*, also blown off course while rounding the Horn. The snow-covered island with its '*sharp and craggy mountains of frightful aspect*' was named Isla de San Pedro, after the saint's feast day of 1st July – the day on which they sailed around the southeast end of the island. Several latitude and longitude positions were noted, and mention made of numerous seabirds, seals and whales.

South Georgia was finally put firmly on the map by the great English navigator Captain James Cook. During the second of his three voyages of exploration aboard HMS *Resolution* (462 tons), Cook circumnavigated the world searching for the 'Southern Continent'. Familiar with the earlier report of Isla de San Pedro he hoped that the island would prove to be part of Antarctica.

On 14th January 1775, an '*island of ice*' was sighted by Midshipman Willis as the ship approached the western end of the island. Next day, Cook daringly sailed *Resolution* northwards through Stewart Strait, the two kilometre wide passage separating the Willis Islands from 'Bird Isle' to the east, so named by Cook '*on account of the vast numbers that were upon it*'.

Cook worked his way eastwards along the north coast of mainland South Georgia and early on the morning of 17th January hove-to at the entrance to Possession Bay. A boat was lowered, and with a midshipman and the three ship's naturalists Johan Forster, George Forster and Anders Sparrman, Cook was rowed to a small inlet in what is believed to be Prince Olav Harbour, '*perfectly sheltered from the swell, and where the land formed a long projecting point*'. The party made three landings here and Cook displayed the colours and took possession of the Country in his Majesty's name under a discharge of small Arms – '*To the utter amazement of the seals and penguins, the inhabitants*', wrote George Forster.

Proceeding along the coast, Cook was not impressed by the view: '*the inner parts of the country were not less savage and horrible. Not a tree was to be seen*'; but he still hoped that this was the long-sought 'Southern Continent'. It was not until *Resolution* rounded the southernmost promontory and Cook found himself looking northwestward along the coast to the point where they had arrived five days earlier, that he realised his Continent was only a narrow island about 170 km long. He named it the Isle of Georgia and – not surprisingly – called the promontory Cape Disappointment.

THE SEALERS

In an age when explorers were looking for new lands to exploit, Captain Cook found little to report of commercial value at South Georgia. However, the account of his voyage, published in 1777, described numerous seals and triggered the first wave of exploitation of the island's natural resources.

Fur seals were taken from South Georgia's beaches in vast numbers, a 'goldrush' in which the competition for the high value pelts brought sealers in their hundreds to the island. Hailing mostly from England and the United States, the early sealers arrived in ships of 60-150 tons and worked the coast in shallops – small sailing boats of 30-40 tons which plied back and forth between the mother ship and the seal rookeries.

A fur seal's fur is much denser than that of other seals. As in other mammals, it consists of two kinds of fibres: long, coarse guard hairs and short, fine under-fur. In fur seals, the under-fur sprouts in clusters of 20-40 fibres – four times the density of other seals. Initially, the cargoes of skins were taken to China where the fur was shaved off and felted for use in winter clothing. The value of the pelts was greatly increased in 1795, when Thomas Chapman discovered a way of removing the guard hairs without damaging the valuable under-fur.

A sealer's day was spent slaughtering fur seals – irrespective of age and sex – with clubs and lances, then flensing, salting and stacking the pelts before loading them on board. Parties of men would be put ashore to live a precarious, uncomfortable life in rough shelters – an upturned boat, a canvas awning or a cave. Traces of some of these camps may still be seen on South Georgia.

In the 1800-01 season, Captain Edward Fanning of *Aspasia* from New York, obtained a record 51,000 pelts – and his was only one of 17 vessels working at South Georgia that year when a total of 112,000 skins were taken. Not surprisingly, numbers of fur seals soon began to dwindle and the island's population was almost destroyed.

Elephant seals were also hunted and oil extracted from their blubber to supplement cargoes of fur seal pelts and whale oil. A few large cast-iron cauldrons (trypots) in which the blubber was rendered can still be seen on beaches today.

Old-time sealers continued to visit South Georgia until 1913, when the last of the traditional sealing vessels, the American brig *Daisy*, took 1,641 elephant seals. By this time there was a British administration at South Georgia. Sealing licences for an annual quota of elephant seals were issued to the whaling company at Grytviken until the station closed in 1965. This was a strictly regulated industry that operated a closed season during breeding and permitted only adult males to be taken. The high quality of oil and effective management regulations made 20th century elephant sealing a profitable and sustainable harvest.

Robert Burton,
South Georgia
Association

THE EXPLORERS

Robert Burton,
South Georgia
Association

Although Captain Cook's expedition was the first to land at South Georgia and chart the coastline, a more detailed exploration of the island was accomplished by the sealers who arrived in the 1780s. They left few records of their discoveries however, and it was not until 1819 that the first chart of the south coast appeared, compiled by Captain Thaddeus Bellingshausen, commander of the Russian ships *Mirnyi* and *Vostok*. James Weddell, a Scottish sealing captain, who spent a month in Undine Harbour in 1823, wrote about the island's history and wildlife in his account *Towards the South Pole*. He also made the first record of seismic activity – observed as vibrations in a bowl of mercury.

The first dedicated scientific expedition took place in 1882, when the German International Polar Year expedition spent 13 months at Köppen Point in Royal Bay (see page 140). Twenty years later in 1902, Otto Nordenskjöld's Swedish South Polar Expedition aboard *Antarctic* undertook an extensive summer research programme. Among the discoveries made was a fossil mollusc and, significantly, the harbour of Grytviken which the ship's captain, C. A. Larsen, recognised as a suitable site for a land-based whaling station (see page 108).

Through these intermittent visitors' accounts, the island began to reveal its character, but it was the establishment of the whaling stations in 1904 that really opened up the island. In the words of Shackleton, the island became effectively "The Gateway to the Antarctic". With well-stocked stores, workshops and transport facilities, the stations were able to offer their services and hospitality to numerous

ship-borne polar expeditions, among them Wilhelm Filchner's German South Polar Expedition. Working from *Deutschland* in 1911 and 1912, this expedition carried out extensive glaciological, geological and meteorological studies, including balloon flights for studying upper winds and a mapping programme which produced the outline map used by Shackleton and his two companions when they traversed the island in 1916.

South Georgia was not on the original itinerary of Shackleton's *Endurance* (1914-15) but, in the event, the expedition spent a month on the island in 1914, waiting for the ice in the Weddell Sea to clear. During this time a meridian transit beacon was set up at Grytviken to enable whale-catchers to swing their compasses.

In 1912-13, the American ornithologist Robert Cushman Murphy aboard the sealing vessel *Daisy*, mapped the Bay of Isles area and collected bird and seal specimens. In 1928-29, Ludwig Kohl-Larsen, his wife Margit (one of C. A. Larsen's daughters) and photographer Heinrich Benitz, travelled extensively around the island, camping and journeying into the interior and travelling with the sealers, to accomplish a wide range of biological, meteorological and glaciological observations. In 1946, Niall Rankin conducted the first extensive bird survey of the island from his small launch *Albatross,* which was transported from England aboard a whaling factory ship. The whalers and sealers also helped to deploy Duncan Carse and his team of surveyors during the 1951-57 South Georgia Surveys which produced the first detailed topographical map of the island.

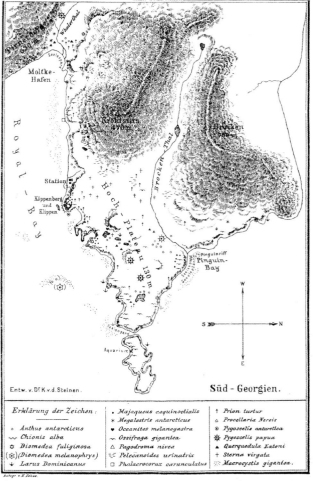

Erklärung der Zeichen:

○ Anthus antarcticus • Majaqueus aequinoctialis † Prion turtur
— Chionis alba ✳ Megalestris antarcticus △ Procellaria Nereis
✿ Diomedea fuliginosa ♥ Oceanites melanogastra ◉ Pygoscelis antarctica
{✿} (Diomedea melanophrys) △ Pagodroma nivea ✿ Pygoscelis papua
↓ Larus Dominicanus ⋈ Pelecanoides urinatrix ▲ Querquedula Eatoni
† Sterna virgata
⋈ Phalacrocorax carunculatus ◉ Macrocystis gigantea.

Ludwig Kohl-Larsen in his klepper boat with King Edward point in the background (*above*) and wildlife distribution map of Köppen Point, Moltke Harbour from the 1882-83 German International Polar Year Expedition to Royal Bay (*right*)
Facing page Filchner's *Deutschland*

35

CARL ANTON LARSEN AND THE WHALING INDUSTRY

Robert Burton,
South Georgia
Association

South Georgia's whaling industry operated from 1904 to 1965, making the island a centre for Antarctic whaling. The Norwegian sealer and whaler Carl Anton Larsen had noted the immense abundance of whales in the Southern Ocean while with Nordenskjöld's 1902 expedition, as well as finding the perfect site for a whaling station at Grytviken. He returned in 1904 with three ships and 60 men to establish the station and begin whaling operations (see page 108). The first whale was caught on 22nd December of that year, starting what was to become a huge and profitable industry that removed a total of 175,000 whales from South Georgia waters.

The main products of whaling were oil and a product called guano. The invention of the hydrogenation process to convert liquid oil into solid fat, enabling whale oil to be used as the raw ingredient for margarine and cooking fat, helped maintain the industry through the 20th century. A considerable amount of oil was rendered from the meat and bones, after which they were processed into meat and bone meal, collectively known as 'guano'. Eventually, endocrine glands were also taken for medical products, and meat extracts and frozen meat were produced.

Initially, whales were so abundant that production of oil was only limited by the capacity of the factory, and other companies soon arrived to share the bonanza. At the peak in 1918-19, when there were six shore stations in operation, the Governor of the Falkland Islands Dependencies, William Allardyce, introduced measures to preserve whale stocks which were already declining. Stations were limited in the number of whale catchers they could deploy, some species were protected and whole carcasses had to be utilised instead of merely stripping off the blubber. Sadly, the development of pelagic factory ships which processed whales on the high seas outside the jurisdiction of the Falkland Islands Government, rendered these regulations ineffective.

Humpback whales bore the brunt of whaling and soon became scarce. As catching equipment improved, blue whales and fin whales became the mainstay of the industry, being the biggest species and thus most lucrative. The processing of whale carcasses also became increasingly efficient through the introduction of new equipment and techniques.

Overproduction and a drop in the price of oil resulted in a temporary closure of whaling stations in the 1932-33 season. After World War II there was an increased demand for whale products but as populations of first blue whales, then fin whales and finally sei whales collapsed, whale catchers had to steam farther afield to hunt. Soon the land-based operations were unable to compete with pelagic

whaling and only Grytviken, Leith Harbour and, for a while, Husvik continued in operation, Grytviken surviving through the addition of elephant sealing and Leith Harbour because it was also a base for factory ships.

Finally in 1963-64, Grytviken and Leith Harbour were leased to Japanese companies that were able to operate more profitably by processing whale meat for human consumption. However even these operations proved unviable and whaling at South Georgia ceased when Leith Harbour finally closed on 15th December 1965.

Above Whale catchers rafted up in
Leith Harbour for the winter
Facing page Carl Anton Larsen (*left*) and
Grytviken whaling station in the 1950s (*right*)

THE *DISCOVERY* INVESTIGATIONS

Robert Burton,
South Georgia
Association

The growth of whaling in the Southern Ocean was such that overexploitation and the subsequent collapse of the whaling industry and whale populations was a predictable outcome. In 1918, in an attempt to counter this, the British Government set up a committee to investigate the preservation of the whaling industry and development of other industries in the Falkland Islands Dependencies which embraced South Georgia, the South Sandwich, South Orkney and South Shetland Islands.

The committee recommended a programme with two main lines of investigation to be funded from the tax on whale products. The first was a detailed survey of the seas around South Georgia. Scientists realised that sustainable management of whale stocks required an understanding of the whales' environment, especially their food supply – principally krill, which itself depends on planktonic algae. These in turn depend on the physical and chemical composition of the ocean and its currents. Captain Scott's ship *Discovery* was purchased and re-equipped as an oceanographic research ship, which arrived at South Georgia in February 1926, and the programme was named the *Discovery* Investigations.

Meanwhile, the second line of investigation, aimed at unravelling the intricacies of whale growth and reproduction, had already started at Grytviken. A prefabricated laboratory, Discovery House, was erected on King Edward Point in early 1925 and for six years a small team of biologists collected specimens from the whale carcasses as they were being dismembered on the plan at Grytviken. Shore-based biologists also studied the birds and seals of South Georgia, and inshore hydrographic surveys were carried out from the launch *Alert*.

When *Discovery* was found to be not entirely suited for oceanographic work, she was replaced in 1929 by the specially designed *Discovery II*. Another ship *William Scoresby* completed the fleet. She was built along the lines of a whale catcher and was employed to mark whales by firing numbered metal darts into their blubber. Of some 5,000 darts fired, only 370 were recovered from the bodies of whales on the flensing plan, but they helped to demonstrate the migrations of whales between feeding grounds and breeding grounds.

The *William Scoresby* also joined in the ocean surveys, initially around South Georgia, the Falklands and the South Shetlands, but later around the entire Southern Ocean. From these cruises, which continued at intervals until 1951, the system of currents and the nature and ecology of the Polar Front and the Southern Ocean were determined.

The *Discovery* Investigations were a milestone in the study of the natural environment and the 38 volumes of scientific reports turned the Southern Ocean from a virtually unknown wilderness into one of the best-studied regions on the planet. But the main objective, managing the whale stocks, was not achieved. With whaling driven by economics rather than by conservation science, the whales were ultimately over-hunted and the industry collapsed.

DUNCAN CARSE AND THE SOUTH GEORGIA SURVEYS 1951-57

Another major milestone in the unveiling of South Georgia was the South Georgia Surveys of 1951-57, driven by the inspiration, energy and organising skills of one man: Duncan Carse.

At the age of 19, Carse signed on as a square rig apprentice on *Archibald Russell*, before joining *Discovery II* for a series of voyages as part of the *Discovery* Investigations. In November 1934, when *Discovery II* was in Port Stanley, Carse transferred to the British Graham Land Expedition's vessel *Penola*, becoming the youngest member of the party. *Penola* over-wintered in the ice off the west coast of the Antarctic Peninsula and during the winter sledging journeys, Carse discovered a life-long passion for polar exploration.

On his return to England in 1937, Carse began a broadcasting career with the BBC. There, after a spell in the Royal Navy during World War II, he took on the character role of Dick Barton, Special Agent, in 1949, and became a household name for a generation of radio listeners.

Carse's passion for polar exploration never diminished, and in 1950 he set about investigating the possibility of a '*small, inexpensive and useful expedition*'. It was thus that the South Georgia Surveys began, with the principal aim of carrying out pioneering exploration and surveys of an essentially unmapped island. Carse organised and led four expeditions (1951-52, 1953-54, 1955-56, 1956-57). During the first three seasons he and a team of geologists and surveyors, living under canvas, surveyed most of the island's interior, including the

route taken by Shackleton. In the final season, Carse completed the coastline mapping aboard the sealing vessels *Albatros* and *Dias*.

Entirely funded by private support, the expeditions were outstandingly efficient, both logistically and scientifically. The results appeared in 1958 as a Directorate of Overseas Survey map of South Georgia (DOS 610, scale 1:200,000 with contour intervals of 500 feet). An impressive document for its time, it became the standard topographical reference map for the island and was crucially important during the 1982 conflict.

Carse returned to the island in 1961 to experiment on the difficulties of living alone in complete isolation. He took out a 10 year lease on 10 acres of land at Undine South Harbour, for a rent of one shilling a year. Early on the morning of 20th May, after three months in 'Amow House', the hut he built on the shore of a sheltered cove near Ducloz Head, a series of huge surge waves demolished the camp. Carse managed to salvage enough equipment to survive the long winter until he was able to make contact with a ship some 116 days later.

Duncan Carse died on 2nd May 2004 aged 90. His name and those of other members of the South Georgia Survey team live on amongst the island's peaks and glaciers: Bomford Peak, Price Glacier, Mount Paterson, Heaney Glacier, Trendall Crag, Mount Baume, Mount Cunningham, and of course Mount Carse, the 2,300 m peak that dominates the southern end of the island.

ESTABLISHING BRITISH ANTARCTIC SURVEY RESEARCH

*David Walton,
British Antarctic
Survey*

Isolated islands often provide interesting scientific opportunities and South Georgia has proved to be no exception. In 1882–83 the German International Polar Year Transit of Venus Expedition established the island's first research station at Köppen Point in Royal Bay and began the first systematic scientific examination of the island, investigating magnetics, geology and botany.

Daily meteorological records began in 1905 after the establishment of Grytviken whaling station and continued, unbroken, until 1982. By the 1950s a proper survey of the geology of the whole island was complete, while research on elephant seals had provided a sustainable basis for harvesting.

In the 1960s plant surveys were initiated with the support of British Antarctic Survey (BAS – then known as the Falkland Islands Dependency Survey, or FIDS) and work undertaken on the reindeer, fur seals and albatrosses. In 1969, BAS took over the management of the island on behalf of the Falkland Islands Government. New research facilities were established at King Edward Point and Bird Island. Science studies were expanded to include the physics of the upper atmosphere, magnetic fields, ecology of terrestrial plants and invertebrates, elephant and fur seals, alien species (rats, reindeer and mice), albatrosses and petrels, and a new inshore and offshore marine biological programme established. The biologists mapped the flora and fauna of the island in detail, ringed thousands of birds to study populations and migrations, and even fenced the reindeer grazed vegetation to see how quickly it could recover. International initiatives stimulated a study of changes in the island's glaciers and more detailed surveys of geology, geomorphology and seismic monitoring.

Annual BAS marine science cruises commenced in 1980 as part of the United Kingdom's contribution to the International Southern Ocean BIOMASS programme, and provided much of the scientific basis for the initiation of Convention on the Conservation of Antarctic Marine Living Resources (CCAMLR) which came into force in 1982.

Inevitably the interruption caused by the conflict in 1982, and subsequent military occupation of King Edward Point affected some of the BAS work on the island. Mainland programmes in particular were limited to some summer biology studies (mostly at Husvik) on terrestrial ecology and fresh water lakes in the 1990s. In contrast, bird and seal research at Bird Island became year-round after 1982. This complemented the marine science cruises and made Bird Island the leading Southern Ocean site for marine predator-prey-environment interactions, particularly in the context of advice on the sustainable management of resources. Today, the BAS marine research programme includes work on fisheries management at the new fisheries laboratory at King Edward Point for the Government of South Georgia.

SOUTH GEORGIA, A DIPLOMACY CASE

South Georgia hit the headlines in 1982 when Argentine forces invaded the island and were expelled 22 days later by the British Navy – a conflict closely associated with the Argentine invasion of the Falkland Islands that took place at the same time.

The British claim to sovereignty over the island is based on Cook's discovery and formal claim in 1775 with subsequent promulgation, occupation, and effective administration. The earliest indication of an Argentine claim was in 1927, although it was not formally stated until 1938. Argentine claims are difficult to interpret in isolation, being inextricably linked with similar claims over the Falkland Islands, several Antarctic islands, and part of the Antarctic continent. Throughout the 1940s and 1950s several attempts were made by the British to solve the dispute through the International Court of Justice but all were rebuffed by the Argentines.

Fifteen years after the last whaling station was abandoned a scrap metal dealer, Constantino Davidoff, based in Buenos Aires, obtained a contract from the owners, Christian Salvesens Ltd., to remove metals from specified abandoned whaling stations on South Georgia. The contract, apparently a purely commercial transaction, was signed in 1979, but by late 1981 it was evident that the Argentine Navy had become involved. On 17th March 1982, an Argentine naval vessel *Bahia Buen Suceso* with scrap metal salvage workers aboard arrived at Leith Harbour without clearing customs and immigration at King Edward Point, the island's administrative centre, and an official protest was made by the local British Magistrate. Then on 24th March, the Argentine naval presence was reinforced with the arrival of two Argentine naval vessels carrying helicopters and over 200 troops.

With British Forces preparing to defend the Falklands, 22 Royal Marines were deployed on South Georgia aboard the ice patrol vessel HMS *Endurance*, landing on 30th March at King Edward Point. On 3rd April, the Argentines attacked King Edward Point, and after it was surrendered, all British personnel were captured and transferred to prison in Argentina, and eventually released in Uruguay.

In response, Operation Paraquat was launched to regain the island. On 25th April, after both air and ground reconnaissance operations, a demonstration of British naval artillery resulted in the capture of the submarine *Santa Fé* and forced the Argentines at King Edward Point to surrender. The following day the Argentines at Leith Harbour also surrendered and all Argentine personnel were deported. Unfortunately, during the brief conflict three Argentines were killed and both sides suffered injuries. The stations were inevitably damaged during the conflict and although mines and booby traps were cleared, the dangers of unexploded ordinance from both Argentine and the 20 years of subsequent British military occupation remain.

The sovereignty dispute over South Georgia persists. Argentina continues to make diplomatic assertions which Britain continues to reject; to this day all maps published in Argentina are legally required to include 'Islas Malvinas' (Falkland Islands) and 'Isla San Pedro' (South Georgia) as part of the country.

The crippled *Santa Fe* alongside the jetty at Grytviken in 1982

R. K. Headland,
Scott Polar
Research Institute

41

STAMPS

The history of South Georgia stamps is inextricably linked to the island's political status. Until 1944 Falklands Islands' stamps were used, albeit postmarked with a South Georgia cachet. Subsequently, definitive stamps were issued for the Falkland Island Dependencies, which included South Georgia, South Orkneys and Graham Land (the Antarctic Peninsula), with the smaller denomination stamps overprinted with the name of the Dependency, e.g. South Georgia. Finally, on 17th July 1963, following ratification of the Antarctic Treaty (1962) which separated British Antarctic Territory from the Falkland Islands Dependencies, South Georgia received its first independent set of definitive stamps. Issues of 'South Georgia' stamps were then issued at intervals until in 1985. In that year the island's status changed once more as it became a UK Overseas Territory, together with the South Sandwich Islands, resulting in an alteration in the stamp's designation. Today, two or three First Day Covers for 'South Georgia and the South Sandwich Islands' are issued annually and a set of definitive stamps is issued every two years.

Flora and Fauna, 1998
COMMEMORATIVE SHEET

Birds, 1999
DEFINITIVE SET

Marine Life, 2001
DEFINITIVE SET

tourism

SOUTH GEORGIA
& the South Sandwich Islands

Official First Day Cover

26 SEP 1998

Tourism, 1998
FIRST DAY COVER

CURRENT ACTIVITIES

37p

Adult & Crèche

SOUTH GEORGIA &
THE SOUTH SANDWICH IS.

GOVERNMENT ADMINISTRATION

*Sarah Lurcock,
Registrar and
Deputy Post Master,
King Edward Point*

The South Georgia Government's resident representative on the island is the Government Officer who is responsible for the administration of all shipping, tourism and other government matters at South Georgia. Pat Lurcock has held this post since 1992, and accompanied by his wife Sarah, lives and works at King Edward Point for about eight months of each year. Initially, accommodation consisted of two spartan rooms in the now demolished Post Office, and meals and entertainment were shared with the British military garrison also stationed at the Point. Today, two Government Officers rotate the post and enjoy a modern three bedroom home, Carse House, and since the departure of military forces in 2001, their neighbours are the British Antarctic Survey (BAS) personnel who live in Everson House at the nearby research station.

Since 1992 there has been a huge increase in shipping, as tourism and fishing activities have expanded annually. In 2003 there were 225 vessel visits to the island, involving over 260 harbour entries by cruise ships, yachts, fishing vessels, cargo ships, fishery patrol vessels, research vessels and warships. The Government Officer carries out customs clearance, prepares invoices for harbour dues, issues Visitor Permits, briefs vessel staff on environmental codes of conduct and safety, and collects the Post-Visit Reports which provide the government with information about visitor activities.

Fishing-related enterprises are the island's main source of income and take up most of the Government Officer's time, even during the southern winter fishing season, when both Government Officers are working. Fishing vessels wishing to operate within the 200 nautical mile Maritime Zone must purchase a licence from the government. Prior to the commencement of fishing each vessel is inspected at King Edward Point to ensure that they are equipped to fish within the laws and regulations that protect both the fish stocks and the broader ecosystem components. Each day, the Government Officer records the position, effort and catch information from every fishing vessel in the Maritime Zone and presents regular reports and statistics to the fishery managers.

Other resident administrative posts are those of Magistrate, Registrar, and Deputy Post Master. The post of Magistrate is filled by the BAS base commander, and the two Registrars (Sarah Lurcock and Pauline Carr, who is also one of the curators at the Museum) have officiated at two weddings in the last few years.

Philately is currently the third greatest income earner after fishing and tourism, and collectors worldwide buy the attractive South Georgia stamps. The Post Office at King Edward Point opens for residents and visitors on request. The Post Office first started operating during the whaling era and has been in continuous operation since 1909, with the exception of a short interruption to services in 1982 during the Argentine occupation. Mails are carried to and from the Falkland Islands by visiting vessels before being forwarded to destinations worldwide. With mail often taking several months to reach family and friends, the recent e-mail connection has been a revolution for island residents.

TOURISM

Tourism is the second largest commercial industry at South Georgia, although, in terms of annual income for the government, it barely equals the price of one fishing licence. Tourists first started visiting the island as early as 1924, when the steamship *Fleurus* sailed regularly from the Falkland Islands with mail, cargo and passengers for South Georgia offering return

A zodiac landing for cruise ship passengers (*above left*) and mountaineers descend a steep snow ridge (*above right*).
Facing page RRS *Ernest Shackleton* alongside the jetty at King Edward Point

'tourist' tickets. *Fleurus* was replaced by *Lafonia* in 1934 and a series of other vessels until the service was terminated in 1971 with the final voyage of *Darwin*.

1970 saw the start of modern day tourism to South Georgia when *Lindblad Explorer*, a vessel built specifically for polar tourism, made her first visit to the island. She remained the only passenger ship in the region until the 1977-78 season when *World Discoverer* began operations in the Antarctic. By the

Denise Landau and John Splettstoesser, International Association of Antarctica Tour Operators (IAATO)

early 1990s several other small cruise ships were including South Georgia on their Antarctic itineraries, and more and more of the island's hidden corners were discovered by nature lovers from all over the world.

Tourism underwent rapid expansion after 1991 when a number of Russian ice-strengthened vessels became available for tourism charters. Since then, the number of ships and visitors has increased annually. Currently, there are over 40 visits by cruise ships each season carrying a total of around 3,500 passengers.

A small number of visitors also arrive by yacht. The first was Bill Tilman and his crew on *Mischief* who sailed into Grytviken in 1967, followed by the French cutter *Damien* in 1971. Today a dozen or so small sailing vessels each season tackle the windy week-long passage from the Falkland Islands. Some are private cruising yachts, others are charter yachts on hire to expeditions for a range of activities including scientific research, mountaineering, filming, kayaking and diving as well as tourism.

Inevitably, the increase in tourism activities has brought about changes in visitor management as the South Georgia Government fulfils its commitment to protecting the wildlife and natural environment of the island according to its Environmental Management Plan Policies. The tour operators, as a

group, have made those policies easier to implement through the establishment of the International Association of Antarctica Tour Operators (IAATO), formed in 1991 to advocate, promote and practice safe and environmentally responsible private-sector travel to the Antarctic. IAATO members, numbering over 70 in 2005, endorse the numerous guidelines developed for Antarctic tourism which they apply equally to South Georgia. These guidelines, or codes of conduct, pertain mainly to activities around wildlife, for example maintaining appropriate distances from nesting birds, marine mammals in the water and seals hauled out ashore, awareness of fragile vegetation, and vulnerable species such as nesting albatrosses and giant petrels.

Management of visitors ashore is done by experienced tour operator staff guiding small groups, an integral part of the educational experience that is a key feature of tourism in South Georgia. Positive visitor response is evident, as testified by the generous financial support given to related wildlife causes and the South Georgia Museum at Grytviken.

Above Yacht *Damien* at King Edward Point during her first visit to South Georgia in 1971
Left Kayaking is an increasingly popular activity for visitors

SOUTH GEORGIA FISHERIES

Fishing first started around the island in the late 1960s. Initially krill, marbled rockcod and icefish formed the bulk of species caught, but from the late 1980s toothfish were targeted, and today there are currently four regulated commercial fisheries, for crab, krill, icefish and toothfish.

Fishing activities come within the jurisdiction of the Government of South Georgia and the South Sandwich Islands, which enforces a 200 nautical mile Maritime Zone around the island. In conjunction with the international Commission for the Conservation of Antarctic Marine Living Resources (CCAMLR), conservation measures are set to keep catches within sustainable limits and to reduce the impact of fishing on the marine ecosystem.

The revenue generated by fisheries licences is the single most important source of income for government. It is used to implement fishery management measures, to provide scientific observers for the fishing vessels and to fund fisheries research and surveillance by Fisheries Protection vessels. This surveillance prevents South Georgia waters being targetted by illegal fishing vessels.

Research is undertaken by two organizations: the Marine Resources Assessment Group Ltd. (MRAG) and British Antarctic Survey (BAS) (see page 48). MRAG provides advice to the government on the levels of catch and distribution of fishing effort. It also operates the scientific observer programme and in partnership with commercial vessels and BAS, it investigates techniques that can be used to reduce the incidental catch of bird and mammal species.

The most valuable fishery is for Patagonian toothfish. This species can grow up to 2 m in length, and is much prized in the Far East and North America. Fish are caught on longlines during the winter months, from May to September (see page 52). In contrast, icefish (maximum length 45 cm) are caught by pelagic (midwater) trawling which takes place during the summer, predominantly on the South Georgia and Shag Rocks continental shelf where the species feeds principally on krill. The fish are sold whole, mainly in the Baltic states. Krill is the third major commercial fishery, again using pelagic trawls. This fishery takes place in the winter months, with the catch being used mainly as a food product for the aquaculture industry.

Fishing at South Georgia can be daunting. Rough seas, driving snow, icing up of decks and rigging, icebergs and sub-zero winter temperatures are the norm and even in summer, conditions can be tough for the crew employed with the baiting, setting and hauling of lines, gutting, packing and freezing of the catch and carrying out running repairs. There may be up to 18 vessels in the fishing fleet, with a multinational crew of around 40 individuals on each vessel.

The South Georgia toothfish industry was recently awarded Marine Stewardship Council accreditation

*David Agnew,
MRAG Ltd*

FISHERIES RESEARCH AT KING EDWARD POINT

*Mark Belchier,
British Antarctic
Survey*

The South Georgia Government funds an extensive programme of research in support of the development and sustainable management of South Georgia's valuable fisheries. Shore-based biological research is carried out by the British Antarctic Survey (BAS) at the Cook Laboratory, the applied fisheries research facility at King Edward Point (KEP). BAS and the Marine Resources Assessment Group Ltd. (MRAG) conduct joint biennial research cruises for the government and represent the United Kingdom at the scientific meetings of the Commission for the Conservation of Antarctic Marine Living Resources (CCAMLR). These surveys provide government with fisheries stock assessments, and monitor changes in both commercial and non-commercial fish stock size and population structure.

BAS employ three scientists who spend a period of over two years conducting research at the fisheries laboratory at KEP. They are supported by five logistics and maintenance personnel including a doctor who provides emergency cover for fishing vessels, and

are joined each summer by visiting scientists from the United Kingdom. The research facility consists of a well-equipped laboratory, freezer facilities, specimen store, a wide range of computing facilities and a purpose-designed inshore fisheries research vessel. The laboratory also runs an aquarium for studying the growth and reproduction of specimens obtained from both the offshore commercial fishery and inshore waters in Cumberland Bay.

The research is targeted towards the main commercial species harvested within South Georgia's Maritime Zone. Two fish species, the Patagonian toothfish and mackerel icefish, are currently fished around the island along with the euphausiid crustacean, krill. There are also unexploited stocks with the potential to support new commercial fisheries including 'stone crabs' and squid. The scientific team works year round at KEP collecting data on many aspects of the biology and ecology of species that are taken by the fishery, and those that have the potential to support a fishery in the future.

Research falls broadly into three areas: studies of the biology of fish caught by commercial fishing boats, monitoring of the ecology of commercially important species found within the Cumberland Bay fjord system and research surveys of South Georgia's commercial fishing grounds.

This essential research provides the required information to develop, manage and sustain these resources under the framework established by CCAMLR.

Detailed biological sampling of commercial catches is undertaken with the cooperation of MRAG observers onboard fishing vessels. Information on the life cycle and population structure of fished species is obtained by collecting data on size, sex, age, reproductive status and diet. In addition, research is conducted on aspects of the ecology of non-target (or bycatch) fish and invertebrate species, which are caught incidentally by fishing vessels. This information is necessary in order to assess the impact of fishing on both target and non-target species – the ecosystem approach to fisheries management.

Biological and oceanographic sampling of Cumberland Bay waters is continued throughout the year working from the inshore fisheries research vessel. The temperature and salinity of the seawater in the bay are measured on a monthly basis. Plankton sampling using a fine-meshed plankton trawl provides an opportunity to examine the early life history stages of many local fish species including the mackerel icefish. Studying the occurrence and abundance of fish larvae within

the bay makes it possible to accurately assess when spawning takes place and how the timing of spawning events changes from year to year. Static gill nets are also deployed throughout the year in Cumberland Bay in order to sample the local adult fish population. A large variety of different fish species are caught, including several species of Antarctic rock cod, icefish and adult Patagonian toothfish, showing that they are present within the bays of South Georgia as well as at the great depths (1,000 m) offshore where the fishery operates.

Above left krill
Above (top to bottom) sea anemone;
giant isopod; nudibranch

SEABIRD AND SEAL RESEARCH AT BIRD ISLAND

Seabird and seal research at Bird Island started in the 1950s with Nigel Bonner (fur seals) and Lance Tickell (albatrosses), the latter developing a four year (to 1964) United States funded programme which built the original base hut, known as Lonnberg House. British Antarctic Survey (BAS) research commenced in 1971 and the Bird Island field station became a year-round facility after 1982. Over the last 30 years more than 100 scientists have worked at Bird Island, mainly in field programmes led by the late Peter Prince under the overall direction of John Croxall.

In that time Bird Island has become recognised as one of the world's leading sites for seabird and fur seal research. The research addresses three interlinked themes. Firstly, the status and trends of the main penguin, albatross and seal species which are being investigated by means of long-term population studies designed to investigate how long-lived animals maximise their survival and reproductive performance under the rigorous conditions of the Southern Ocean. For albatrosses, these studies have, regrettably, become exemplary evidence of long-term declines in populations, largely attributable to

John Croxall,
British Antarctic
Survey

the effects of longline fishing (see page 52). Most of South Georgia's albatross populations have halved over the last 20 years, and, even if the human-induced mortality were to end today, it would take some 50 years for the populations to recover. In the meantime, much has been discovered about how albatrosses operate their unusual (biennial) breeding cycles and what characterises successful breeding birds. In contrast, the population study of fur seals has followed one of the most spectacular recoveries from near-extinction – from a population of a few hundreds in the 1930s to over 3 million today.

The second theme looks at the ways in which seabirds and seals exploit – and depend on – the marine environment at South Georgia. BAS pioneered research into diet and feeding ecology, and more recently, in conjunction with satellite tracking, has investigated exactly where and when individuals feed. It is now understood, in some detail, how the abundance of krill, squid and lantern fish around South Georgia is responsible for the extraordinary diversity and abundance of top predators – and that these predators can exert powerful local influences on their prey. For example, the increase in king penguin populations is believed to relate to characteristics of lantern fish, their exclusive prey, although understanding how this link works, remains for future research. Similarly, the recovery of fur seals is thought to be due to their exceptional ability to exploit Antarctic krill, but only recently has it been discovered that this may be at the expense of macaroni penguins, also krill specialists, which are declining markedly.

Thirdly, long term monitoring programmes have been initiated to quantify changes in survival and reproductive performance of key species and to provide evidence of system change. In the late 1980s these programmes, involving two penguin and three albatross species and Antarctic fur seal, were the basis and later the backbone of the Commission for the Conservation of Antarctic Marine Living Resources (CCAMLR) Ecosystem Monitoring Programme. Nowadays nearly 50 variables are measured annually at Bird Island to provide a "state of the ecosystem" assessment.

Increasingly the research at Bird Island has become central to the management of marine resources around South Georgia under the auspices of CCAMLR. In addition to providing information on the condition of top predator communities, the Bird Island data now contribute vital information on the population dynamics of krill and icefish (sourced from seal and penguin diet samples) as well as new insights into the distribution and abundance of squid (from albatross samples). BAS research and advocacy was fundamental to CCAMLR's development of strict regulations to reduce the bycatch of seabirds in the longline fishery for toothfish: in just five years this was reduced from 6,000 to less than 30 birds per year.

The challenge for the future is not just to ensure that all this research continues, but that its results are incorporated into new ways of managing the region's marine resources on which the future of South Georgia – as well as its penguins, petrels, seals and albatrosses – depends.

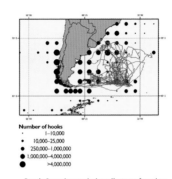

Number of hooks
- · 1–10,000
- 10,000–25,000
- ● 250,000–1,000,000
- ● 1,000,000–4,000,000
- ● >4,000,000

South Georgia wandering albatross foraging tracks during chick-rearing (males in blue and females in red), and their overlap with longline fisheries in the South American sector. BAS, unpublished data.

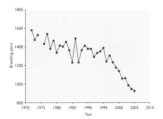

The decline in the wandering albatross population at Bird Island. BAS, unpublished data.

LONGLINE FISHERIES AND SEABIRDS

Keeping South Georgia's albatrosses off the hook

Text adapted from the presentation 'Albatrosses and Longline Fisheries' by Graham Robertson

The seabirds of the Southern Oceans, and albatrosses in particular, never fail to delight visitors with their beauty, abundance and effortless flight. For those lucky enough to be able to spend time ashore at their nesting grounds, the spectacular courtship display of South Georgia's wandering albatrosses is an unforgettable experience. Less evident to the visitor however, is the thinning out of the breeding colonies and emptying of the skies as the existence of several species is threatened.

Victims of the world's longline fisheries, tens of thousands of albatrosses and petrels are killed at sea every year when they unwittingly seize baited hooks intended for catching fish. Longline fisheries catch fish by using a long piece of rope to which are attached thousands of baited hooks. There are two types of longlining: surface longlining and bottom longlining. Surface longlines are suspended about 200 m beneath the surface, and a single line can exceed 100 km in length, carrying 3,000 baited hooks on 40 m-long branch lines (spaced 50 m apart). They are used mainly by Japanese, Korean and Taiwanese vessels to catch tuna and swordfish on the high seas, particularly in the Indian Ocean, and by inshore fishing vessels in domestic fisheries around the world.

Bottom longlines are made of heavier ropes than surface longlines, and usually have weights attached to the lines to make them sink to depths of up to 2,000 m. The lines are 10–30 km in length and carry far more hooks than the surface longlines – up to 40,000 hooks are set and hauled in each day. Bottom longlines are used to catch deep water fishes, for example cod, sable fish and halibut in northern

hemisphere waters, and ling, hake and Patagonian toothfish in the Southern Ocean.

As longlines are paid out from vessels, seabirds are attracted to the baited hooks, and also to the offal from processed fish which is thrown overboard during fishing. Both activities encourage seabirds to congregate in their thousands around the vessel, diving for the baited hooks. In this way, thousands of birds are hooked or entangled in gear, drawn underwater and drown.

Every year an estimated three billion baited hooks are set by longliners in the oceans inhabited by vulnerable seabird species. The richest waters for both fisheries and birds occur around the margins of continents and islands such as New Zealand, South America, South Africa and South Georgia, and also at ocean fronts where water masses mix and upwell.

But how do we know that seabird populations are declining? Irrefutable evidence comes from research programmes on sub-Antarctic islands around the world. At South Georgia, British Antarctic Survey scientists have been monitoring albatross populations of Bird Island (one of the world's richest seabird breeding sites) for over 25 years, and the results are alarming: the island's grey-heads are disappearing at over 2% each year, black-brows at nearly 5%, and the most recent data for wanderers indicate a 4·5% annual decline. These scientists also report seeing birds regurgitating hooks and line, and observers on fishing vessels tally the numbers of birds killed during fishing operations.

There are several effective measures available to fishers to help reduce seabird mortality. These are:

• Fishing at night
• Flying streamer lines during line setting operations to scare seabirds away from baits
• Adding weights to longlines to ensure that the lines sink fast
• Processing fish offal onboard or expelling it in a manner that does not attract seabirds
• Setting lines underwater through a pipe

The first four of the above measures are mandatory for longlining in oceans south of the Polar Front, a region where all fisheries activities are managed by the Commission for the Conservation of Antarctic Marine Living Resources (CCAMLR). The Commission also requires that an observer be on board all vessels to document fish and seabird catches. Strategies implemented by the Government of South Georgia include the adoption of all CCAMLR measures as well as limiting longlining operations to the winter months when most vulnerable seabird species have finished breeding and departed from South Georgia

waters. Closing the fishery in summer has reduced the number of seabirds killed to less than 30 each year, and in 2005, not a single albatross was caught by licensed vessels fishing within the Maritime Zone.

However, for a masterful flier like an albatross the world is a small place and 'safe' maritime zones are only a tiny part of their back yard. Satellite tracking studies of albatrosses from South Georgia reveal that the birds fly around the entire Southern Ocean, and significantly, feed along the coasts of Argentina, Uruguay, Brazil, South Africa and Australia in areas of longlining activity.

Currently, the efforts of South Georgia and other governments to reduce the impact of fisheries on seabirds in their national waters are outweighed by the devastating impact of the illegal, unregulated and unreported fisheries that are widespread on the high seas. Vessels from these fisheries are thought not to use any measures to prevent seabird mortality, with the result that hundreds of thousands of seabirds (mainly white-chinned petrels, shearwaters, albatrosses and giant petrels) are killed annually. Persuading governments to take the necessary steps to ensure that illegal vessels are not allowed to operate and that high seas longline fishing practices become more 'seabird-friendly' is paramount in the campaign to keep seabirds off the hook.

Wandering albatross drowning on a longline fishing hook (*above*) and longlining for Patagonian toothfish (*below*) *Facing page* Giant petrels and black-browed albatrosses feeding at the stern of a fishing vessel

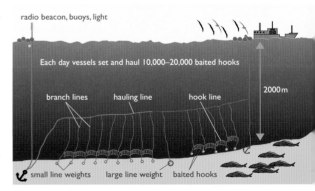

radio beacon, buoys, light

Each day vessels set and haul 10,000–20,000 baited hooks

branch lines   hauling line   hook line

2000 m

small line weights   large line weight   baited hooks

53

THE APPROACH TO SOUTH GEORGIA

Everyone reaches South Georgia by sea. While many view this crossing with trepidation, the ocean voyage can be as exciting as the arrival. For the first day or so after leaving the Falklands, albatrosses, petrels and shearwaters often accompany the ship, skimming the waves and riding the air current on their long wings. Then, about mid-passage, there is a noticeable change: the air becomes cooler, the sea temperature drops as much as 5°C, and often mist forms. These changes mark the crossing of the Polar Front. Different bird species appear in abundance: blue petrels and clouds of small, ghostly grey-white prions that flit just above the surface of the water, providing an identification challenge for even the keenest birder.

Black and white chequered cape petrels swarm around the ship and occasionally a group of hourglass dolphins surf the waters at the ship's bow. But perhaps the most exciting event is the first sighting of an iceberg. These bergs are myriad pieces of former floating ice shelves which have broken away from the Antarctic Continent. They come in many forms, from dramatic castellated bergs to huge, flat-topped tabulars, some over half the size of South Georgia. Beautiful though these ice sculptures are, they pose a serious hazard to navigation. On board the look-out watch is often doubled as the bridge keeps a wary out eye out for 'growlers' – small lumps of ice which are virtually invisible among the waves.

If time and daylight permit, the ship may sail close by Shag Rocks. These isolated rocky islets lie 240km west of South Georgia. They are the highest points of a continental fragment of Gondwana, and are composed of finely banded grey-green schists, a very different rock type to any seen on South Georgia. The steep rise in the surrounding ocean floor and the associated nutrient-rich upwellings sustain an abundance of seabirds, fur seals and whales. Orcas and minke whales are commonly seen; also the occasional southern right whale, fin whale and humpback whale and even blue whales.

As the vessel closes in on the island, macaroni, king, gentoo and chinstrap penguins porpoise alongside en route to and from their feeding grounds, and fur seals stop to look inquisitively at their new visitors. Then at last, the island appears, ice-covered mountain peaks shimmering above the horizon, magical in their isolation, surpassing all expectations.

KEY TO SITE MAPS

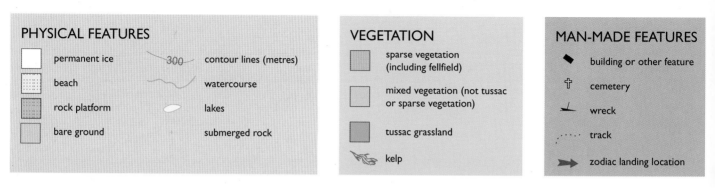

PHYSICAL FEATURES

- permanent ice
- beach
- rock platform
- bare ground

- *300* contour lines (metres)
- watercourse
- lakes
- submerged rock

VEGETATION

- sparse vegetation (including fellfield)
- mixed vegetation (not tussac or sparse vegetation)
- tussac grassland
- kelp

MAN-MADE FEATURES

- building or other feature
- † cemetery
- wreck
- ······ track
- zodiac landing location

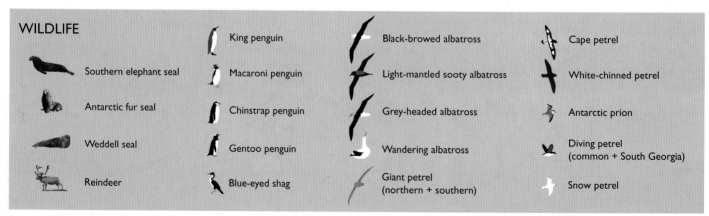

WILDLIFE

- Southern elephant seal
- Antarctic fur seal
- Weddell seal
- Reindeer

- King penguin
- Macaroni penguin
- Chinstrap penguin
- Gentoo penguin
- Blue-eyed shag

- Black-browed albatross
- Light-mantled sooty albatross
- Grey-headed albatross
- Wandering albatross
- Giant petrel (northern + southern)

- Cape petrel
- White-chinned petrel
- Antarctic prion
- Diving petrel (common + South Georgia)
- Snow petrel

56

ELSEHUL

54° 01'S 37° 59'W

Once known as Paddock Cove, after an early sealing captain and possibly one of the first visitors to enter the harbour in the 1780s. The name Elsehul (Norwegian for Else Cove) dates back to around 1905 when the first whalers re-discovered the bay.

FEATURES

▸ Three species of penguins and three of albatrosses
▸ Fur seals breeding in huge numbers
▸ Trypots
▸ Ideal for zodiac cruising

POINTERS

▸ Landings are not recommended during the peak of the fur seal breeding season
▸ Minimise use of vessel lights at night to prevent bird strike

LOCATION AND MAIN FEATURES

Situated at the northwestern extremity of South Georgia on the eastern side of Paryadin Peninsula, Elsehul is a beautiful little harbour with an astonishing array of wildlife. It is the only visitor site on the island where colonies of black-browed and grey-headed albatrosses can be viewed from zodiacs within the protection of sheltered inshore waters.

Entered between Post Rock and Cape Pride, Elsehul is reasonably sheltered in all but winds from the northerly quarter, although it may be subject to swell of varying intensity depending on wind direction. It is often the first site visited by cruise ships arriving from Stanley, and yachts commonly drop anchor on the western side of Inner Bay.

LANDFORM AND HABITAT

Rock and scree slopes dominate the landscape, rising to the knife-edged summit ridges of Paryadin Peninsula above the western shores of the harbour. Comprised of folded sedimentary rocks of the Cumberland Bay Formation, the massive 400 m high ramparts of Paryadin Ridge front the full force of westerly gales and form a backbone along the entire 7 km length of the peninsula from Cape Alexandra south to Cape Paryadin. The climate here is typical of the northwest end of the island, being much wetter, windier and cloudier than the 'banana belt' of the central north coast region.

The harbour is about 4 km long and 300 m wide at its narrowest point, with the cauldron-shaped basin of Inner Bay forming a sheltered arena for zodiac cruising to view the wildlife. Close west, just outside the entrance, is a delightful little bay, Joke Cove, backed by very steep fur seal-trampled tussac slopes and a razor-back ridge terminating in the 50 m high headland called The Knob. A low-lying narrow neck of land about 350 m wide and covered in fur seal-worn tussac and muddy gullies, is all that separates Elsehul from the long stretch of beach in Undine Harbour. To the east, flows one of South Georgia's largest rivers, Hope River whose headwaters lie in the 800 m high icy summits of Snow Peak. It meanders across Hope Valley's 7 km of gravel plain and between tussac and moss-covered hills, passing dark-watered tarns before entering the sea in Undine Harbour.

The shores of Elsehul are steep-sided and dotted with hundreds of black-browed and grey-

Below Grey-headed albatross
Facing page Joke Cove with Elsehul beyond

headed albatrosses nesting on the cliff and tussac ledges. Below them, the rocky foreshore is packed with fur seals, which climb as high as 100 m altitude to find a quiet tussac bog to sleep on. They have transformed the landscape, creating a morass of rounded bare tussac bogs and mud which in places has eroded away to bare rock. This erosion is also exposing relics from the past: trypots and ruins of early sealers' huts. Once surrounded by tussac, they are now clearly visible on the mud and rock on the main landing beach.

WILDLIFE

The abundance and diversity of wildlife at this site is remarkable. Three species of penguins and three of albatrosses nest within sight of the shoreline, as do giant petrels, shags, sheathbills, elephant seals and fur seals. White-chinned petrels, cape petrels, Wilson's storm-petrels, brown skuas, South Georgia pintails, wandering albatrosses and Antarctic terns pass over the harbour as they return to their nest sites on the higher slopes and inland tussac areas. Norway rats, introduced long ago by early sealers, have eliminated pipits and the small tussac-burrowing petrels which would once have been as numerous here as they are on nearby rat-free Bird Island.

On the approaches to the harbour, huge numbers of albatrosses are often seen rafted up on the water. Nearly 400 pairs of black-browed albatross and over 1,500 pairs of grey-head nest on the tussac slopes at Post Rock at the western entrance point to Elsehul. More grey-heads (nearly 700 pairs) nest on the headlands either side of Joke Cove, in company

with several dozen pairs of blue-eyed shags on The Knob, and there are another 600 pairs of grey-heads scattered along the southern and eastern shores of Inner Bay and out to Pull Point where there are about 600 pairs of black-brows nesting on the outskirts of a colony of several thousand macaroni penguins. This side of the bay is also favoured by light-mantled sooty albatrosses which can often be heard calling from the cliff ledges and wheeling overhead in perfect synchronised flight.

Gentoo penguins nest by the hundred on the tussac slopes between Elsehul and Undine Harbour, making their way patiently through the fur seals and elephant seals at the head of Inner Bay. There is usually a group of moulting king penguins on the little southern beach, an outpost of the small breeding colony tucked away among the fur seals in Joke Cove. In the early spring, these beaches are the domain of breeding elephant seals and their attendant scavengers, the brown skuas and giant petrels. By November the entire foreshore is covered in fur seals, as the first territorial bulls haul out, followed by females and then their newborn pups.

HUMAN HISTORY

Since its discovery by sealers in the late 1700s, Elsehul has been one of the most frequently visited sites on the island. The main landing beach area on the western side of Inner Bay was ideal for sealing operations, being protected from swell, with plenty of fresh water and level ground for setting up tryworks and campsites. The narrow isthmus provided a safe shortcut across the island, and boats were often

dragged overland to the south coast rather than risk the treacherous waters of Bird Sound. Today, the outlines of at least two huts are discernible near three large trypots, reminders of that period 1790–1820 when virtually all of South Georgia's fur seals and a large proportion of its elephant seal population were killed. In all, at least 1·2 million skins were taken by the time the sealing captain and explorer James Weddell visited Elsehul in 1823 aboard *Jane*. Anchored in Undine Harbour in company with his escort, the tiny cutter *Beaufoy* commanded by Matthew Brisbane, Weddell and his men explored the area for over a month, searching for seals to complement their cargo. Fresh greens – probably the native burnet – and tender albatross chicks were added to the menu to restore the men's health, and much-needed repairs were made to the vessels.

Over a hundred years later, in 1928, Ludwig Kohl-Larsen spent several weeks exploring the area from a campsite in Coal Harbour, east of Undine Harbour and encountered only one fur seal during his entire stay!

During the 1970s, Elsehul's growing fur seal population was the focus of a British Antarctic Survey research programme. A small field hut was built on the western side of Inner Bay next to the trypots and was a familiar sight to summer visitors until its removal in 2003.

VISITING THE SITE

Weather and swell permitting, zodiac cruising is definitely the best option for visitors to Elsehul. The steep muddy terrain, narrow beaches and above all, the sheer density of wildlife and especially fur seals (this is one of the densest fur seal breeding beaches at South Georgia) mean that there is little room left for visitors to land safely and comfortably. During the breeding season in particular – from November through to late January – the shoreline is a writhing mass of seals, bulls, cows and pups all jostling for limited space on the beach and little inclined to move aside for visitors. If you do venture ashore towards the end of the summer, be aware that the tussac is usually full of fur seals, and be prepared for mud – deep, sticky, pungent mud. The constant trampling by fur seals has killed off much of the tussac and created a maze of brown slippery mounds laced with a network of mud-filled channels. In contrast, a zodiac cruise along the shore from Joke Cove to the macaroni colony near Pull Point provides some of the best wildlife viewing that South Georgia has to offer.

Facing page A black-browed albatross with chick on its pedestal nest (*top*) and a macaroni penguin stretches its flippers on emerging from the water (*bottom*)

Below Fur seals near the trypots

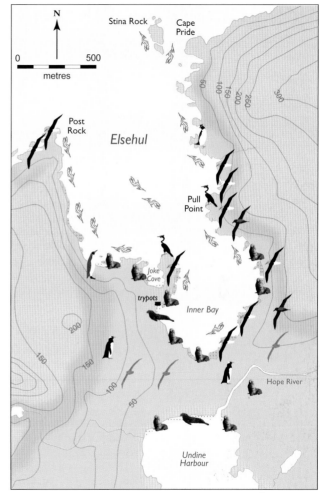

PRION ISLAND

Named by Robert Cushman Murphy, after the Antarctic prions he found nesting there in 1912.

FEATURES
▸ Wandering albatrosses
▸ South Georgia pipits

POINTERS
▸ Special rules apply: refer to the special rules and a Government Code of Conduct
▸ Landings are not recommended during the peak of the fur seal breeding season
▸ Until a walkway is constructed keep to the rock gully and avoid walking on damp soft areas and tussac with burrows

LOCATION AND MAIN FEATURES

Prion Island lies in the Bay of Isles towards the west end of South Georgia's northeast coast. It is a site of high environmental sensitivity and exceptional conservation value, and one of the few rat-free tussac islands remaining along this rat-infested coastline. It is also an important breeding site for wandering albatrosses and the endemic South Georgia pipit, and has extensive areas of fragile vegetation, including stream margin flushes and tussac areas burrowed by petrels. Being rat-free, the island has abundant populations of vulnerable seabird species, including common diving petrels, white-chinned petrels, giant petrels and Antarctic prions. South Georgia pintails, light-mantled sooty albatrosses, fur seals and elephant seals are also regular breeders. For these reasons, a special code of conduct applies to all visitors who land on the island.

LANDFORM AND HABITAT

The island is a little over 1 km in length and 500 m wide. A 50 m high central plateau runs the length of the northern half of the island, flanked by tussac-covered slopes that descend to 15–25 m high sea cliffs on both the east and west coasts. The island is entirely covered in tussac, with small areas of damp *Deschampsia* grassland on the plateau area and some scattered *Festuca* on some of the better-drained west-facing slopes. The tussac on the slopes behind the landing beach is a conspicuously darker shade of green than on the upper slopes due to nutrient enrichment, a sure indication of fur seals which occupy this area in large numbers throughout the summer. The 75 m long shingle beach on the east coast guarantees all-weather landings, being protected to seaward by a network of low-lying rocks, reefs and kelp beds which dampen most swells. At the north end of the beach, a rock gully leads uphill between the tussac bogs to the main wandering albatross nesting sites.

WILDLIFE

Wandering albatrosses nest predominantly on the upper slopes of the northern half of the island. Like the remainder of South Georgia's wandering albatross population, the number of breeding pairs has declined by nearly 30% in the past 20

years. Currently, the total breeding population is about 60 pairs, about half of which nest on the island in any one year.

A colony of about 1,000 pairs of gentoos occupies a low rise behind the landing beach and in some years, a small number nest on the hilltop at the south end of the island. The penguins access these areas from the south end of the landing beach, plodding up a narrow rock gully through dense tussac. Southern giant petrels and a few northern giant petrels nest on the plateau area, often in close proximity to the wandering albatrosses. White-chinned petrels burrow in the steep-sided tussac gullies along the west coast. Common diving petrels are found on the tussac slopes along the northern

Above South Georgia pipit
Right Wandering albatross on nest

Facing page South Georgia pintail

cliffs, while Antarctic prions burrow in many of the small tussac knolls. The coastal cliffs are ideal nest sites for light-mantled sooty albatrosses, and there are usually several pairs in residence on both the east and west coasts. South Georgia pipits can be seen all over the island. The parents are incessantly on the wing as they feed chicks in their snug nests beneath the tussac. It is not unusual to see these birds on the landing beach, foraging for kelp flies and amphipods along the shoreline in company with South Georgia pintail. Elephant seals breed here, and haul out to moult in deep muddy wallows in the tussac close by. From November to January, the landing beach is covered in breeding fur seals, and each year increasing numbers venture further and further inland, encroaching on the nest sites and display areas of the wandering albatrosses.

HUMAN HISTORY

Robert Cushman Murphy, an American ornithologist from the American Museum of Natural History, spent the summer of 1912-13 at South Georgia studying the island's wildlife. Working from the whaling brig *Daisy*, he established a campsite on Start Point on the mainland opposite Prion Island and collected bird specimens while the vessel's crew hunted elephant seals. On several occasions he rowed out to nearby Albatross Island in his small dory (named *Grace Emeline* after his wife) and discovered wandering albatrosses, pipits and prions, all nesting in great abundance.

Daisy was the last of the 19th century sealing vessels to visit the island. Many such vessels were

63

wrecked at South Georgia, and a large wooden spar on the beach at Prion Island is possibly the remains of one of these (*Lovely Nancy*) lost in the Bay of Isles in 1820. In later years, elephant sealers from Grytviken would occasionally call in to collect wandering albatross eggs and fat fledglings, a practice that continued until the early 1960s when all whaling ceased.

In 1999, a monitoring programme was established at Prion Island and Albatross Island to investigate the interactions between visitors, fur seals and wandering albatrosses, and to record the annual population and nest distribution of albatrosses, the number of visitors and the impact of fur seals on plant communities. Since monitoring began, the wandering albatross population on both islands has declined from over 230 pairs to less than 190.

VISITING THE SITE

A special code of conduct applies to all visitors landing at Prion Island. Landings are permitted only on the east coast beach, where the government intends building a jetty and boardwalk. Until completion of the boardwalk, a water-worn rock gully at the north end of the landing beach offers the easiest access route between the beach and the wanderer viewing areas. This 200 m long track becomes extremely wet and muddy towards the top where it joins a level plateau area. Repeated trampling of damp soft ground by visitors creates visible and long-lasting damage to vegetation, and in those tussac areas burrowed by petrels, trampling also damages the underground network of tunnels and nest chambers as the ground collapses underfoot. Damage to vegetation and seabird-nesting habitat can be avoided by walking in the rock gully or on the better drained adjacent tussac areas, flagged by someone with local knowledge to avoid seabird burrows.

In westerly winds, there is a reasonable anchorage for yachts close inshore on the east coast of the island. However, access to the designated landing beach on the east coast of the island, may be affected by easterly winds or a heavy northerly swell.

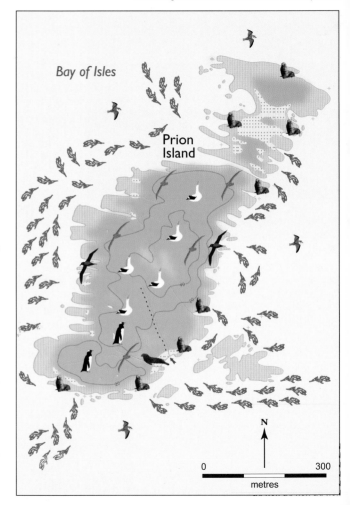

Bay of Isles

Prion Island

N

0   300
metres

Wandering Albatrosses

Richard A. Phillips,
British Antarctic
Survey

No visit to South Georgia would be complete without seeing wandering albatrosses, be they gliding effortlessly across the ocean, sitting serenely on the nest, or dancing gracefully in front of a prospective partner. These magnificent birds are the archetypal ocean travellers. With an average mass of 9-10 kg in males and 7-8 kg in females, wandering albatrosses are by no means the heaviest flying bird, but their average wingspan (over 3 m) is greater than in any other species. They also have an exceptionally low divorce rate, most birds pairing for life. Incredibly, a few birds banded as breeding adults by the pioneer seabird ecologist Lance Tickell on Bird Island in 1958, were still present in 2005. Given a minimum age at first breeding of eight years (the average is 11 years) these individuals must be at least 55 years old!

During the breeding season, wanderers travel enormous distances, returning on average only every 20 days to take their turn incubating the egg, or every four to five days to feed the chick. While at sea the prey are reduced to a lipid-rich stomach oil with a very high calorie content thus maximising the energy provided to the chick when the adult does return. To withstand such long periods without food, chicks accumulate prodigious quantities of fat and when eight months old can weigh 50% more than adults and easily survive for several weeks if poor feeding success delays the return of the parent. Low chick feeding frequencies and high fasting capabilities are fairly typical of other albatrosses and petrels, but the wandering albatross is unusual in being one of the

few species that breed during the austral winter. It also has amongst the longest chick-rearing period (278 days) of any bird.

Pioneering studies using satellite-transmitters at Bird Island in the early 1990s revealed that during incubation, some adults were travelling as far as 7,500 km on foraging trips lasting less than two weeks. They can clearly fly extremely rapidly, and more recent research using highly accurate, miniaturized geographical positioning system (GPS) loggers confirms speeds over short distances of up to 135 km/hour. Birds at sea follow typically zigzag flight paths, continuously changing speed and direction in order to maximise the energy gained from the prevailing wind. Indeed, attachment of external heart-rate loggers (which provide an instantaneous measure of energy expenditure) shows that when travelling with favourable tail or side winds, wanderers use only slightly more energy while at sea than they do sitting around at the colony. The most energetically expensive activities are take-offs and landings, and this explains why birds seen from a ship usually alight on the water only to take food from on, or just below, the surface. Interestingly, wanderers are very poor divers, never reaching depths greater than 60 cm. This contrasts with black-browed and grey-headed albatrosses, which can dive to depths of 5-6 m, and light-mantled sooty albatrosses that are capable of reaching up to 12 m.

The diet of wandering albatrosses is extremely diverse, including a range of crustacea (Antarctic krill in particular), fish and a wide variety of squid.

Rather conveniently for researchers, shortly before fledging the chicks regurgitate boluses containing all the squid beaks accumulated throughout the long nestling period, presumably to reduce weight as much as possible before their first flight. Analysis of boluses collected at Bird Island between 1989 and 1999 reveals no less than 26 different species of squid and one octopus. The distributions of these prey range from subtropical to Antarctic waters, which parallels the huge overall foraging range (from 25°–68°S and 15°–86°W) of breeding adults tracked from Bird Island over the last 15 years.

There are also some intriguing gender differences in both foraging distribution and diet. Results from the very first satellite-tracking study and subsequent research using GPS loggers indicate some rather subtle distinctions depending on breeding stage. Females have a slight tendency to forage in more northerly waters, particularly during incubation, and are much less likely to travel through the Drake Passage. During brood-guard, one parent must always be in attendance at the nest to reduce the risk of predation, and also of starvation, as the chick has not yet developed sufficient fat reserves to tide it over between parental visits. Adults are therefore constrained to feed much closer to the colony, and differences between the sexes are then much more clear-cut. Males feed predominantly on the local South Georgia shelf and shelf-slope. By comparison, females utilise these habitats to a lesser extent, instead feeding routinely in oceanic waters from 51°-56°S. This is corroborated by dietary analyses: during brooding, males consume large amounts of Patagonian toothfish presumably obtained as discards from long-line fishing vessels in the local area, whereas females feed on a much greater diversity of fish and squid.

One unfortunate consequence of this is that females are more likely to be caught by long-line fishing vessels (targeting tuna in particular) in subtropical waters. Males, by comparison, are more vulnerable to incidental mortality associated with the higher latitude, demersal longline fishery for Patagonian toothfish. Despite the efforts of the South Georgia Government and the Commission for the Conservation of Antarctic Marine Living Resources (CCAMLR) to ensure a well regulated fishery, breeding numbers of wandering albatrosses in South Georgia continue to decline (at 4·5% per annum since 1997). This is partly because adults are still vulnerable to mortality in long-line fisheries outside of the South Georgia maritime zone in their breeding and wintering ranges (the latter extending throughout the Southern Ocean as far as Australia), and also because the previously very high mortality of young birds means that recruitment rates of new breeders are now insufficient to maintain a stable population. Until the bycatch mitigation measures used in South Georgia's waters become the norm on all vessels wherever they are fishing, the future prospects of wandering albatrosses, as for virtually all albatrosses throughout the world's oceans, appear bleak.

Above Grace under pressure – wandering albatrosses, like many seabirds, use the uplifting air currents to glide and soar with minimum energy expenditure

1

Courting wanderers engage in elaborate courtship dance sequences

2

A male approaches a female with a rolling gait, hump-backed and moving its head from side to side

5

Circling around the display nest, wings outstretched

6

Sky-calling, neck-rolling and pointing are accompanied with ...

3

Billing, where birds approach and touch each other, is often accompanied by low groans

4

The birds begin their dance sequence

7

... bill vibration which produces a drumming sound and frequently ends in bill-snapping

8

Finally the bird closes its wings and bill-snaps as its partner circles with head flagging

SALISBURY PLAIN

54° 03'S 37° 19'W

Named by John Chaplin (Royal Navy surveyor 1926–1930 for the Discovery Investigations) who probably saw in the bleak expanses a likeness to the place of the same name in England.

FEATURES

▸ Second largest king penguin colony at South Georgia
▸ Breeding elephant seals
▸ Breeding fur seals
▸ Grace and Lucas Glaciers

POINTERS

▸ Landing dependent on swell conditions
▸ Take care to avoid elephant seal harems
▸ Avoid approaching and disturbing groups of moulting kings
▸ Minimise use of vessel lights at night to prevent bird strike

LOCATION AND MAIN FEATURES

Salisbury Plain is a vast expanse of glacial outwash plains on the southern shores of the Bay of Isles, 50 km from the western extremity of the island. Formed by the retreat of the Grace Glacier, and now covering over 2 km², it is the largest area of level ground at South Georgia - large enough to have warranted a detailed survey in 1984 as a possible aircraft landing site. Its seaward margin is a 2 km long grey sand beach that runs from Start Point east to the vicinity of a large king penguin colony. The beach continues uninterrupted for another 3 km to Luck Point, and in places forms a sand bar separating the sea from a large lagoon that was created during the retreat of the Lucas Glacier. One of South Georgia's largest elephant seal breeding populations hauls out here, and every year, fur seals continue to spread along the beach from Start Point where they were first seen breeding in the late 1980s.

LANDFORM, CLIMATE AND HABITAT

South Georgia is barely 10 km wide in the Bay of Isles, and the 1,000 m high peaks of Mt. Ashley offer little protection from the strong westerlies that blow in from King Haakon Bay on the other side of the island. Rapid changes in weather are not uncommon as winds are channelled down the Grace and Lucas Glaciers hit the Salisbury Plain coastline with gale-force fury.

The two glaciers are separated by prominent rock outcrops and bluffs that descend nearly to the coast from the inland ridges and peaks of Mt. Ashley. A swiftly flowing river carries sediment-laden meltwater from the Lucas Glacier past the eastern side of the bluffs and on warm days fills the bay with plumes of milky coloured water, particularly after heavy rain. The river is usually packed with moulting kings from the nearby colony which nestles at the foot of the bluffs. Tussac surrounds the colony area and also the headlands at Start Point, but otherwise the plain is a barren wasteland of sparsely scattered lichens, mosses and various grasses, intersected by a myriad of streams and pools extending inland to the retreating snout of the Grace Glacier.

WILDLIFE

King penguins are everywhere, literally as far as the eye can see. The rivers and streams are lined with them, there are tens of thousands dotted all over the plain, and with no fixed entry and exit point to the sea, they may occupy the full length of the beach. First estimated at 350 pairs in 1912, the colony, like many at South Georgia, has undergone a phenomenal increase, and is now estimated at around 60,000 pairs, with as many as 250,000 birds in total on the beach during the moult period.

During the winter months, the penguins have the beach to themselves, but by early spring, hundreds of elephant seals haul out, forming dozens of tight-knit harems. By December, swarms of weaners dot the beaches, snoring gently in the sand, and the wallows at the back of the beach below the king colony, are jammed with noisy smelly moulting adult seals. At this time also, breeding fur seals are well established, the majority of pups being born on the shores of the little coves at Start Point. There are several pairs of brown skuas nesting on the slopes above the king colony, and a large colony of kelp gulls on the plain below the Lucas Glacier.

HUMAN HISTORY

The abundant elephant seal population in the Bay of Isles was well known to sealers. As late as 1877 – after nearly a century of hunting – Heinrich Klutschak on board the New England sealer *Flying Fish*, noted that '*the Bay of Isles, Bird Island and Willis Islands are the fur seals' chief breeding grounds*', although in fact by then, there were few fur seals left on the island. Elephant seals however, were hunted right up until the end of sealing in 1964, and the Salisbury Plain area was a prime sealing beach. It was also well

Right Each king penguin colony encompasses all stages of the breeding cycle
Facing page Two snoozing elephant seal weaners

known for its king penguin colony, and a number of scientists travelling on sealing vessels were landed at the site.

Robert Cushman Murphy spent 10 weeks in the Bay of Isles. He compiled a chart of the bay and recorded several place names on it, including the Grace Glacier for his wife. He also kept a detailed notebook of his journey, later published as *Logbook for Grace*, and containing an excellent account of sealing. Throughout his time at the encampment, the weather was typical of the Bay of Isles: his tent was blown over several times and even with an oil stove it proved difficult to keep warm. Nevertheless, he succeeded in amassing a comprehensive set of skins and several skeletons for the two institutes' collections.

Twelve years later Ludwig Kohl-Larsen and his wife Margit, accompanied by film-maker Albert Benitz, also camped at Start Point in similarly trying conditions, studying and filming the kings for seven weeks. Two separate ornithological expeditions, one led by Dr. C. Gibson-Hill and the other by Niall Rankin, visited the colony in 1946, but it was some years before the king penguin breeding cycle was fully understood. In 1953 Bernard Stonehouse and Nigel Bonner spent 14 months studying the birds. They lived in a hut in Ample Bay, 2km west of Start Point. Bonner investigated fur and elephant seals while Stonehouse concentrated on the kings. In addition, they collected 12 months' of meteorological data. Although living in relative isolation (the nearest inhabited whaling station was over 60km away in Stromness Bay), the two men had occasional visits

71

Below The Salisbury Plain king penguin colony is situated at the foot of a tussac-covered bluff, and spills out onto the former glacial plain

Facing page The glacial outwash plain below the Grace Glacier, with the king penguin colony in the top left hand corner and Lucas Glacier beyond

from whalers and sealers, partly social and partly to collect penguin eggs – the visitors were grateful, no doubt, that Stonehouse took the trouble to mark the date of laying on each egg, enabling them to select the freshest.

VISITING THE SITE

Landings at Salisbury Plain are very dependent on sea and weather conditions – it is quite common for strong gusts of wind to come whistling down the glaciers with little warning, and rubber boots are a must as there is usually surf on the beach and the ground very wet and muddy, especially around the colony. Once ashore, walk slowly and quietly to the top of the beach before heading towards the king penguin colony, taking care not to stumble across seals hidden amongst the masses of penguins crowded along the shore. Regardless of where you land – it could be anywhere from directly below the colony if the surf permits, or near Start Point if more shelter is needed – the best route is to follow the top of the beach until directly in front of the colony. Short-cuts across the tussac and grass areas invariably end up in streams or wallows. Head up the western face of the bluffs for a stunning view of the colony from above – but be prepared to make a detour as skuas nesting in the area will vigorously defend their nests. Lastly, do take the time to sit or lie on the beach too, where dozens of curious king penguins are likely to investigate any newcomers, even pecking at boots and gloves.

Tern Island

Start Point

Dot Island

N

0   500
metres

Bay of Isles

Salisbury Plain

Grace Glacier

Lucas Glacier

PRINCE OLAV HARBOUR

54° 04'S 37° 09'W

*Known variously as Crows-
nest Harbour, Crow's
Harbour, Crew's Harbour
and Rat Harbour to 18th and
19th century sealers, and
Port Gladstone to the early
British administration, the
harbour was renamed Prins
Olaf-Hafen by Norwegian
whalers in the early 1900s, in
honour of the Crown Prince
of Norway.*

FEATURES

▸ Hulk of *Brutus*
▸ Whaling station
▸ Fur seals

POINTERS

▸ Not suitable for landings
during the fur seal
breeding season
▸ Beware of submerged
debris when cruising in the
vicinity of the station
▸ Drive slowly in Elephant
Lagoon

LOCATION AND MAIN FEATURES

Prince Olav Harbour is a small sheltered inlet within Cook Bay at the western entrance to Possession Bay. At its head lies the whaling station of Prince Olav Harbour. The harbour is effectively made up of three arms (South, North and East Bays), in the middle of which is Brutus Island, a tussac-covered islet surrounded by kelp. Elephant Lagoon lies on the south side of the harbour and is connected to the sea by a narrow channel called Carl Passage.

This is a site steeped in history from the early days of exploration. First explored by Captain James Cook, the harbour was well-known to sealers and 20th century whalers. Their legacy – a jumble of rusting orange-coloured buildings and derelict machinery in the whaling station, the hulk of the three-masted ship *Brutus* and the graves on the hillside above – all lend an indefinable atmosphere of mysterious abandon to the harbour, despite the incessant clamour of the many thousands of fur seals that have invaded the site in recent years.

LANDFORM AND HABITAT

The steep scree slopes and jagged summit ridges that enclose the harbour to the west and south, offer some protection from the westerly winds that are channelled through King Haakon Bay on the island's south coast before being forced up over Shackleton Gap – a low ice-covered saddle squeezed between two mountainous massifs of over 1,000 m altitude – and down into

The old whaling station

Possession Bay. The hinterland, while considerably lower in altitude than the Allardyce Range, is nonetheless impressively glaciated, and the region is generally less vegetated than the central northeast coastline. Tussac-covered peninsulas and forelands are not as common here as in the central north coast areas, and the gently sloping, green tussac and moss areas around Elephant Lagoon in particular, provide a welcome contrast to the stark wind-blasted glacial landscape of Possession Bay.

Geologically, the rocks of the area belong to the Cumberland Bay Formation with some spectacular folds visible in the summits above the station. Large numbers of fossils have been found here, the most common being a bivalve mollusc, *Aucellina*, with a few fragments of larger shells, including ammonites, and several microfossils.

WILDLIFE

This is one of the few sites at South Georgia where, remarkably, there is not a penguin colony in sight! Instead, kelp gulls rule the roost, their plaintive calls echoing round the bay as they seek out limpets along the intertidal zone or warn intruders away from their nests.

Fur seals are everywhere, breeding in very high density on all the beaches from Elephant Lagoon right round to the north shore of the harbour. Elephant seals haul out to breed and moult on either side of the Elephant Lagoon isthmus, and at the entrance to the lagoon itself. One or two small harems form in North Bay below the station's freshwater reservoir, and from December till March, a number of moulting seals can always be seen inside the partially collapsed workshop at the south end of the beach fronting the whaling station. Here, for many generations now, seals have piled in two or three deep, covering the broken floorboards in a heaving brown mass of snorting, steaming, stinking flesh and blubber to sleep through the moult in this warmest, most sheltered of wallows.

HUMAN HISTORY

Prince Olav Harbour is one of the most significant historical sites at South Georgia. When Captain James Cook landed in Possession Bay on 17th January 1775 and

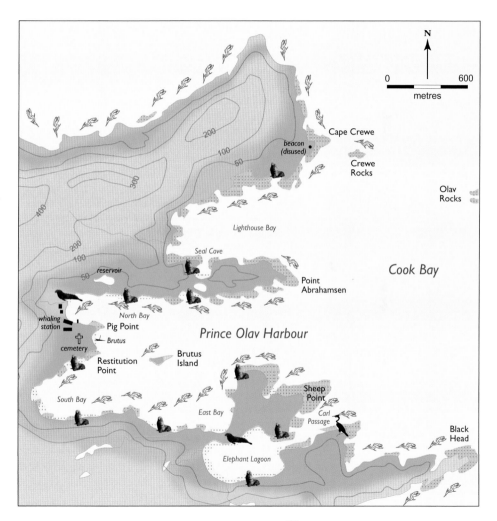

proclaimed the island for England, he may well have stepped ashore in Cook Bay. Although the precise location is unknown, the several firsthand accounts of the event describe a site very like Prince Olav Harbour.

Within 10 years of Cook's account being published, American and British sealers were harvesting the island's elephant seals, fur seals and king penguins. Prince Olav Harbour was the centre of fur sealing operations. It was the safest anchorage for large vessels close to the main rookeries at Elsehul, Undine Harbour and Bird Island. Several trypots, a cutter and a shanty were seen on the landing beach in the harbour in the 1890s and although there are no signs of these today, there are a number of sealers' graves, both marked and unmarked, in the vicinity of the whaling station cemetery above Pig Point. In 1913, a human skeleton, presumably that of a sealer, was found in a cave in the cliffs near Elephant Lagoon. Of particular note is the grave of John Anderson, mate of the schooner *Mary Jane* of New York, who was buried here in 1838, and the copper-sheeted gravemarker (a replica of which can be seen at the South Georgia Museum) bears the inscription '*An honest man*'.

Prince Olav Harbour is also likely to have been one of the centres of spread of Norway rats, which arrived on the first sealing vessels. Heinrich Klutschak, an Austrian traveller on board *Flying Fish* that circumnavigated the island in 1877-78, wrote that there were a few rats at a place he referred to as Rattenhaffen – Prince Olav Harbour.

With the demise of sealing, the harbour lay empty until the arrival of the Norwegian whalers in the early 1900s. The lease for land in the harbour (under the name of Port Gladstone initially) was granted to the Southern Whaling and Sealing Company in 1911. This was the last whaling lease to be issued by the Falkland Islands Government. The company, owned by Irvin and Johnson with offices in South Africa and the United Kingdom, leased the site until 1919, when it was sold to the British company Unilever.

Operations were initially run from the floating factory steamship *Restitution*. The vessel was equipped with the first radiotelegraphy apparatus on South Georgia, and maintained daily radio communications with its two catchers *TWI* and *COJ* (the initials of the owners) which also used carrier pigeons to deliver news of their catch and estimated arrival time to Prince Olav. *Restitution* was stationed in the harbour every summer until she was wrecked near the Isles of Scilly in England on her way south at the beginning of the 1916-17 season. From then on and until the station finally closed in 1931, whaling was purely shore-based. In 1936, the lease was transferred to Christian Salvesen & Co. Ltd. who used the station for 'spares', dismantling some of the tanks and floating them down the coast to Leith – quite a considerable feat of seamanship and rigging skill. The lease was terminated in 1992, when the site, like all other whaling stations, reverted to the South Georgia Government.

The ship beached near Pig Point is *Brutus*. Built in Glasgow in 1883, the vessel first worked for the

Above (top) The replica grave marker of John Anderson bears the inscription 'Iohn Anderson, Mate of Schr Mary Jane of N York, Capt Joseph E Parsons. Died Nov 23rd AD 1838 in this port on board of the Brig Medina'
Above Wreck of *Brutus* on the beach near Pig Point, Prince Olav Harbour

Facing page The cemetery at Prince Olav Harbour

Sierra Shipping Company of Lima, transporting nitrate. She arrived at Prince Olav under tow by four whale catchers from Cape Town and was used as a coaling hulk.

VISITING THE SITE

During the fur seal breeding season, the density of animals on the beaches makes landings difficult and zodiac cruising is recommended and in particular, a visit to Elephant Lagoon. Tucked in behind Sheep Point is Carl Passage, a narrow channel in the cliffs leading to the lagoon. The shores and waters on all sides are packed with seals, so keep your speed to a minimum once you enter the passage. A cruise in North Bay offers the opportunity not only to see seals, but also to take in the atmosphere of the whaling station – beware though, of semi-submerged debris along the shoreline.

Outside the fur seal breeding season, landings are possible on the beach next to the wreck of *Brutus*. A steep, muddy climb through tussac leads to the cemetery, marked by six ornate iron crosses perched precariously amongst the fur seals and tussac bogs on the summit of the ridge above the station. Nearby is a roughly levelled piece of ground sprinkled with cinders from the station furnaces, a football pitch hewn from rock and scree. A short uphill walk through the fur seal-infested tussac, brings you to the top of the ridge overlooking the station. From here, you can see the old path and water pipe line leading to the reservoir and dam. This is a peaceful spot with wonderful views of the station and the distant peaks above the harbour and Possession Bay.

FORTUNA BAY

54° 07'S 36° 48'W

Named after Fortuna, the first whale-catcher to operate out of Grytviken in the early 1900s, this site includes both the Fortuna Bay king colony near Whistle Cove, and the landing beach for the Shackleton Walk, situated on the east side of the bay (see page 94).

FEATURES

▸ The final leg of Shackleton's route across the island
▸ King penguin colony
▸ Elephant seal breeding beach
▸ Sealers' cave
▸ Reindeer

POINTERS

▸ During the elephant seal breeding season, avoid landing close to harems
▸ Avoid disturbing moulting king penguins

LOCATION AND MAIN FEATURES

Entered between Cape Best and Cape Robertson on the central north coast, Fortuna Bay is a 6 km long fjord leading to the heart of South Georgia's rugged interior. At the head of the bay is a spectacular panorama of the island's alpine scenery, from the König Glacier which sweeps up to join the Neumayer Glacier, to the backdrop of massive ice and rock ramparts of the northern faces of Mount Spaaman, Three Brothers, Larssen Peak and Marikoppa.

The western shores of the bay are dominated by the jagged summit outline of Breakwind Ridge. It was here that Shackleton and his two companions made their descent to the beach in Whistle Cove on the final leg of their crossing of South Georgia. Reindeer graze the grassy slopes, and at the foot of a small outcrop at the back of the beach is a sealers' cave. The king penguin colony, one of the main attractions at this site, is situated about 1 km inland from Whistle Cove on the level outwash plain below the König Glacier.

The bay offers reasonable protection for vessels in most weather, and notably, landings are generally possible at Whistle Cove even when most of the remainder of the north coast is affected by onshore surge and swell. Although the coastline of the southeast corner of the bay south of Hodson Point is frequently subject to swell, a series of low reefs and rocky points usually give sufficient protection for landings on the beach close to the start of the Shackleton Walk track (see page 94).

LANDFORMS AND HABITAT

Characteristic folds in the sedimentary rocks at the entrance to Fortuna Bay are typical of the Cumberland Bay Formation and reminiscent of those in Cumberland Bay and Stromness Bay. This coastal region is relatively ice-free, and huge expanses of scree and rock outcrops dominate the summer landscape. On the western shores of the bay, heavily grazed tussac-covered bluffs and *Festuca* grassland merge with rock and scree slopes at about 100 m altitude. Remnant ice and snowfields on Breakwind Ridge feed numerous water-sculpted V-shaped gullies filled with spectacular waterfalls high above the beach. The sharp lines of the ridge contrast with the smooth upward sweep of the König Glacier and the 2 km curve of beach that fringes the head of the bay. About halfway along the beach, a deep and swift-flowing river meets the sea at the end of its 2 km long meandering journey from the inland snout of the glacier. Sprawling the full-width of the valley and laden with morainic debris, this glacier is the source of innumerable meltwater streams that weave their way seaward through a complex landscape of lagoons and gravel outwash plains covered in a sparse carpet of native grasses, buttercup and pearlwort, mixed with introduced species such as annual meadow-grass and mouse-eared chickweed.

Facing page Whistle Cove king penguin colony in Fortuna Bay (*top*) and Fortuna Bay entrance from the sealers' cave in Whistle Cove (*bottom*)

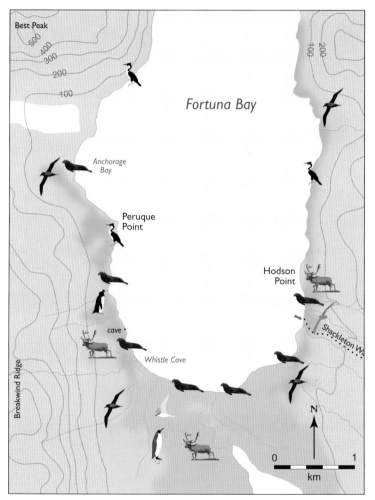

Best Peak

500
400
300
200
100

Fortuna Bay

100
200

*Anchorage
Bay*

**Peruque
Point**

**Hodson
Point**

cave

Whistle Cove

Shackleton Way

Breakwind Ridge

N

0   1
km

WILDLIFE

A king penguin colony of about 7,000 breeding pairs is situated on the level outwash gravel plain below the König Glacier, and about 1·5 km from the landing beach in Whistle Cove. The colony is fringed by nutrient-enriched herbs and grasses, which form a conspicuously bright green area visible from the beach and provide good quality grazing for reindeer. The colony's relatively small size and position on level ground makes it an ideal site for easy viewing of all aspects of the penguins' breeding activities, as incubating birds mingle with chicks and non-breeders. There are several light-mantled sooty albatross nests in this area, and while the nests themselves are difficult to spot and access, pairs can often be seen in courtship flights on the lower slopes of Breakwind Ridge. Small numbers of pintail feed in the streams and pools near the landing beach. A few white-chinned petrel burrows can be found on the tussac knolls above the landing site and there is a small gentoo penguin colony nearby on the hillside above the cave.

Fortuna Bay lies at the westernmost limit of reindeer distribution and small herds of predominantly male animals often graze the slopes above Whistle Cove and the outwash plain in the vicinity of the king penguin colony. Early in the season elephant seal harems occupy the full length of the beach at Whistle Cove, sometimes making the usual landing site impassable. Later in the season the beach is less crowded as the elephant seals move into the wallows between the tussac bogs at the back of the beach. The first fur seal pup was see Whistle Cove in 2001, but the number of breeding fur seals in the area is still low.

HUMAN HISTORY

Fortuna Bay appears to have been visited by most of the early explorers to the island and sealers no doubt made good use of the cave in Whistle Cove. With its low stone wall across the entrance, it would have provided a relatively dry abode for these men who were left ashore for weeks at a time, killing elephant seals and living under very spartan conditions.

In the 20th century, sealers from Grytviken whaling station aboard the sealing vessels *Dias* and *Albatros* regularly visited the huge elephant seal beaches in the bay to take their annual quota of bulls.

VISITING THE SITE

Landings at Whistle Cove are usually possible in all but the roughest of conditions, even when a strong northerly swell is pounding the outside coast. The 1·5 km walk from the landing beach to the king penguin colony is on level ground across the glacial outwash plain and over a few shallow streams. There are often large groups of moulting penguins huddled like breeding birds along the route to the colony. Be sure to take a wide detour around these groups, and be aware that the breeding birds will be using the same route as they come and go from the beach to the colony.

This is an excellent place from which to view Shackleton's route from Breakwind Ridge across the Fortuna Bay beach and up over the pass to Stromness. With king penguins, gentoo penguins, pintail, elephant seals and fur seals in the vicinity of the landing site itself, there is much to be said for simply sitting quietly on the beach letting the wildlife come to you, rather than trekking to the king penguin colony and back.

Burrowing Petrels

Burrowing petrels are the most abundant seabird family at South Georgia. Some very rough estimates from the 1970s have put the total number of breeding pairs at nearly 30 million, of which 22 million were reportedly Antarctic prions. Whatever the precise figure, the numbers of birds that return to the island each summer is truly astounding.

These burrowing petrels are a major link in the Southern Ocean food chain and their food consumption and biomass are believed to rival that of the penguins and albatrosses combined. Arriving and departing from their burrows under cover of darkness, the birds are rarely seen or heard during the day, so that despite their abundance, they remain largely undetected by most visitors. Their underground nesting habitat is a network of tunnels and nest chambers in soft soil, usually beneath the tussac, on scree slopes, or beneath boulders. Nesting underground enables the birds to avoid skua predation and helps to maintain an optimal nest temperature and so maximize the chances of successfully rearing a chick. On the downside, burrow-nesting habitat is susceptible to damage from trampling by both visitors and fur seals as tunnels and nest chambers are liable to collapse at the slightest pressure.

Two hundred years ago, burrowing petrels were probably found in huge numbers around the entire island. Today, however, the smaller species are confined to the rat-free south coast and offshore islands (less than a third of South Georgia's total coastline) and to inland scree and boulder slopes above the limit of tussac grassland and outside the usual range of Norway rats (see page 29). Only the larger **white-chinned petrel** survives in the rat-infested coastal tussac areas. Although rats do take their eggs and young chicks, these larger robust petrels appear to be able to cope with rat predation, and small colonies are found throughout most tussac grassland areas.

White-chinned petrels are the largest of South Georgia's burrowing petrels. Their breeding and migration ranges are globally very large and the

While South Georia diving petrels burrow in scree (*left*), white-chinned petrels excavate large burrows in tussac (*right*)

birds are capable of travelling up to 3,500 km on foraging trips. They can dive to 13 m depth and unlike albatrosses and most other petrels, they hunt both day and night. All these features make them particularly vulnerable to longline fisheries. Globally, it is estimated that several tens-of-thousands of white-chins die annually in the Patagonian toothfish longline fishery, and some scientists consider the species to be equally if not more at risk of significant population declines than the albatrosses. For this reason, the South Georgia Government are conducting a census of South Georgia's white-chinned petrel population in 2005, as part of their commitment to the international Agreement on Conservation of Albatrosses and Petrels (ACAP).

All species of petrels lay a single egg which is incubated for up to two months before hatching. The newly hatched chicks are then brooded for a few days before both parents depart on foraging trips to feed themselves and their chick. Fledging takes place around two months after hatching.

First to return each spring are the **white-chinned petrels**, **blue petrels** and **common diving petrels**. At this time of year, their burrows are often snow-and-ice-bound despite their location on the sunniest and most sheltered north-facing tussac slopes. The period immediately prior to egg-laying is devoted to digging out the burrow, preparing the nest chamber and courtship activities. **Antarctic prions** arrive in October, coming and going from the colonies during their courtship period and until egg-laying begins in mid-December.

Blue petrels are the first to lay their egg, in mid-October. **Common diving petrels** follow about two weeks later, and white-chins have usually started by mid-November. **South Georgia diving petrels**, which burrow in inland scree slopes at up to 150 m altitude, return in late October but do not begin egg-laying until around mid-December when most of the snow and ice has melted from the colony area. **Wilson's storm-petrels**, which may also nest inland and at altitude, are latest of all, laying their eggs toward the end of December. First to fledge are **blue petrel** chicks in late January, followed by **common diving petrels** in early February, then **Antarctic prions** and **Wilson's storm-petrels** in late March and **white-chinned petrels** last of all in mid-April (see the wildlife breeding calendar on page 171).

From late January to March, and particularly on foggy nights, adults and fledglings of the smaller burrowing petrel species are attracted to any source source of bright light – a ship's deck lights, spot-light projectors or lights from buildings. The birds are easily disorientated by the light source, and often collide with windows and vessel superstructures. Advice on how to minimise the risk of bird strike is given on page 12.

The white chin on some of these petrels is sometimes barely discernible

Facing page Early in the season, white-chinned petrels sit at their burrow entrances, calling to their partners (*left*); The blue petrel has a distinctive white band across the tip of its tail feathers (*right*)

TUSSAC NEST SITES
A: Diving petrel
B: Antarctic prion, Blue petrel
C: White-chinned petrel
D: South Georgia pintail
E: South Georgia pipit

living root system

Cross-section: tussac clump

'pedestal'

leaf litter

Cross-section: underground

HERCULES BAY

LOCATION AND MAIN FEATURES

Hercules Bay lies 2·5 km northwest of Cape Saunders, the northern entrance point to Stromness Bay. In calm settled weather the bay offers a temporary anchorage for yachts, and even small cruise ships with local knowledge may venture cautiously inside and drop anchor within the cliff-encircled basin at the head of the inlet.

Zodiac cruises along the inlet's coastline offer unexpected delights: macaroni penguins coming and going from colonies, a sparkling waterfall cascading onto a shingle beach lined with elephant seals and fur seals, extensive kelp beds in crystal clear water and impressive sea caves at the base of 300 m high cliffs patterned with gigantic chevrons of compressed Cumberland Bay Formation sediments, spectacular examples of this geological feature that characterises the Stromness Bay area.

LANDFORM AND HABITAT

The bay is open to the northeast and is a miniature fjord, 1 km long and barely 500 m wide and enclosed by towering cliffs. It is protected to the west by a 500 m high coastal ridge between Fortuna Bay and Stromness Bay, and there are days when its waters lie mirror calm while a fresh westerly breeze is blowing outside. More often though, the surge of ocean swells penetrates right to the head of the bay, and the wind occasionally descends in forceful gusts from the heights of Coronda Peak, blowing the waterfall back uphill.

The encircling cliffs are cloaked in a sparse covering of tussac grass and burnet, and along the shoreline are numerous sea caves, fringed with swirling kelp beds of both *Macrocystis pyrifera* and the less common *Durvillaea antarctica*. The northern shore of the inlet is bordered by low

cliffs topped with gently undulating slopes of reindeer-grazed tussac and *Festuca* grassland.

WILDLIFE

Fur seals and elephant seals breed on the shingle beach at the head of the bay and are occasionally joined by a few moulting king penguins. Overhead, light-mantled sooty albatrosses soar along the cliffs or sit quietly on their nests on the cliff ledges. Not far from the waterfall is a small macaroni penguin colony, best viewed from the zodiac. On the northern shore, a small group of blue-eyed shags honk and twitter away to each other at their colony on the low cliffs, and on the *Festuca* grassland slopes above are southern giant petrels. A small herd of reindeer can often be seen here, hardy individuals that negotiate the high pass separating Hercules Bay from Leith Harbour.

Out towards Hercules Point, areas of dark-green tussac flag the locations of white-chinned petrel colonies and three groups of macaroni penguins. Totalling no more than a few thousand pairs, the groups are offshoots of a large colony (estimated at over 15,000 pairs) about 1 km west of Hercules Bay on a coastline constantly buffeted by the sea. Clearly visible from offshore, the colony is on very steep tussac, and the highest nests are about 150 m above the sea.

HUMAN HISTORY

One of the earliest descriptions of Hercules Bay comes from Frank Hurley who enjoyed a pleasant day here in March 1917 photographing penguins,

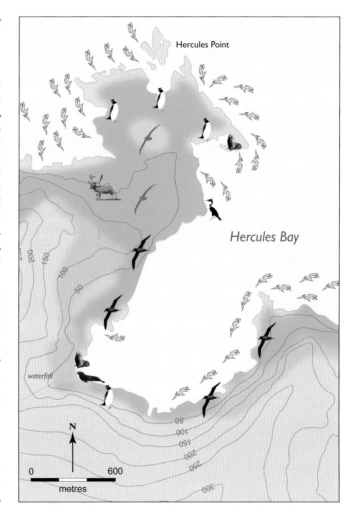

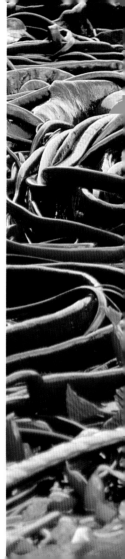

having come round from Leith Harbour on the station motorboat *Matilda,* '*one of the craziest craft I have ever voyaged on*'.

In early February 1928, Kohl-Larsen's team camped for three days on the beach at the head of the bay. After four months under canvas at various places around the island often in bitterly cold and windy conditions, they, like Hurley, were enchanted with the site, likening it to '*a summer resort*'. They found fossils here – later identified as worm tracks and wormholes – and tried their hand at fishing, and with such success that a debate ensued as to whether the fish – a type of rock cod or *Notothenia* – could be caught on a bare hook. It was Kohl-Larsen who provided the first estimate of the size of the large macaroni colony, reckoning between 50-60,000 nesting birds. Interestingly, there was no mention of a colony near their campsite on the beach at the head of Hercules Bay.

In the same year, a young British scientist, L. Harrison Matthews, was just completing his fourth and final season at South Georgia, having explored the island in company with Norwegian whalers and sealers while working for the *Discovery* Investigations. He described whalers from Leith Harbour "egg-picking" at Hercules Bay, climbing the 300 m scree slopes above the whaling station and at the end of the day leaving a dump of eggs (8,000 one year) covered with sacks to keep the skuas away until the station motorboat could fetch them in. Egg-collecting was a tradition that continued until the stations closed in 1964–65, and there are still people who recall with great delight a meal of

fried macaroni penguin eggs.

VISITING THE SITE

Within the relative shelter of the bay, a zodiac cruise offers the best views of the cliffs, birds and seals. Drifting slowly along the coast just outside the kelp, you can see penguins appearing like corks from a bottle on to the landing rocks below their colonies, and in the deep clear waters around you there are often pulsating sparkles of sea combs, and sea butterflies, amphipods and beautiful delicate sandy-pink bivalves hidden among the dark brown fronds of the kelp forest.

Right (top to bottom) Ctenophore; sea butterfly; isopod – all often found in the coastal shallows and kelp forests
Above Macaroni penguins

Facing page Waterfall at the head of Hercules Bay (*left*) and a sea cave along the Hercules Bay coastline (*right*)

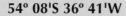

LEITH HARBOUR

54° 08'S 36° 41'W

Named after Leith in Scotland, where the whaling company Christian Salvesen & Co. Ltd. had its head office.

FEATURES
▸ Whaling station
▸ World War II gun emplacement

POINTERS
▸ Do not approach within 200 m of the whaling station
▸ Beware of partially submerged debris when zodiac cruising

LOCATION AND MAIN FEATURES

Leith Harbour is best known for its whaling station, located on the harbour's western shore beneath the scree slopes of the Coronda Peak massif. This is the largest of the South Georgia whaling stations, where the atmosphere of an industrial township is still evident despite 40 years of abandon and dereliction. At its heart is the flensing plan, flanked by rust-coloured factory buildings, warehouses, engineering workshops, accommodation barracks and huge oil tanks which sprawl along the shoreline, bearing silent witness to six decades of whaling.

LANDFORM AND HABITAT

The station is situated on the seaward margin of a steep-sided cirque backed by a rampart of 500 m high rock walls. The ice-clad escarpments of Mt. Antell to the northwest of the station, retain the scanty remnants of a hanging glacier that once filled the headwall of the now ice-free Leith Harbour valley. Braided fluvio-glacial melt-water streams flood the gravel flats along the 2 km length of this valley and collect in a shallow reservoir behind the station dam before making their way seaward past the cemetery and football field on the southern side of the station. On the northern shore of the harbour, steep scree slopes rise to the rocky summit ridge of Coronda Peak. In strong northwesterly gales, gusts of over 100 knots drop vertically from this ridge, lifting the water in a wall of saltspray and sweeping across the harbour before hitting the

station full force. Buildings once anchored down by wire ropes, are now being torn apart under each onslaught of wind and collapse under the weight of each winter's accumulation of snow.

Where the mountain ridge curves southeast towards Harbour Point at the southern entrance to Leith Harbour, scree and rock outcrops give way to *Festuca* and tussac grassland, criss-crossed by streams, seepage gullies and a generous scattering of introduced dandelions, annual meadow-grass and chickweed.

WILDLIFE

Elephant seals and fur seals are the principal inhabitants of the station area, along with the occasional passing herd of reindeer seeking out succulent patches of grass in the shelter of the buildings. Some bull elephant seals occasionally loiter around the jetties, noisily challenging the echoes of their own bellows as their roars reverberate among the timber piles.

A few hundred pairs of gentoo penguins occupy the low hills overlooking the reservoir and cemetery, weaving a path across the football field between the reindeer and fur seals. Pintail are not uncommon, especially in the area near Hansen Point where large elephant seal wallows provide tussac, food and protective cover. A few pairs of kelp gulls usually nest on the point, and can often be seen on the World War II gun and hut ruins, mounting a wary guard on top of the headland.

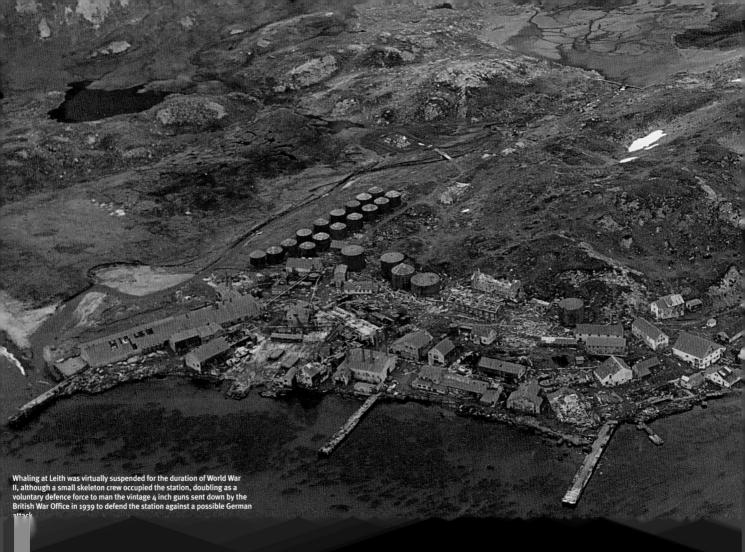

Whaling at Leith was virtually suspended for the duration of World War II, although a small skeleton crew occupied the station, doubling as a voluntary defence force to man the vintage 4 inch guns sent down by the British War Office in 1939 to defend the station against a possible German attack.

HUMAN HISTORY

Leith Harbour, like all of South Georgia's sheltered anchorages, was known to the early sealers, although traces of their presence disappeared once whaling operations began on the site. The harbour was well suited to shipping, having clear approaches from the sea and a steeply shelving shoreline that permitted the construction of deepwater piers for receiving large ships alongside. The Scottish whaling firm Christian Salvesen & Co. Ltd. was granted the lease of the site in 1909 and the factory ship *Starlight*, with two whale catchers *Swona* and *Semla* began operations that summer while construction of the station got underway.

Despite a growing shortage of whales, the company was initially able to maintain economic viability by reinvesting in powerful new catchers, diversifying into the production of meat extract, reducing operational and employment costs, and streamlining the refitting of the company's catcher fleet and pelagic factory ships at nearby Stromness which it had acquired in 1930. Salvesens ceased operating at the end of the 1960-61 season. A Japanese company arranged a five year lease of the

station in 1963–64, but only operated until December 1965, when whaling came to an end for all time.

For over 15 years the station remained silent and unoccupied. The landing of Argentine military forces and subsequent military activity brought in a new era of activity in 1982 as British military regularly patrolled the stations until 2001, when all public access to the whaling stations was prohibited for reasons of safety.

VISITING THE SITE

A visit to Leith Harbour is a unique opportunity to experience a glimpse of life at a whaling station. A zodiac cruise along the waterfront provides good views of the flensing plan, and its surrounding cluster of blubber, meat and bone cookeries and workshops. Also visible are tons of rusting machinery and materials left near the main jetty by the Argentine scrap metal merchant Constantino Davidoff in 1982.

The station manager's villa and office, once the hub of station life, now perches precariously close to the encroaching waterfront at Coronda Pier while at the head of the harbour, known as 'Jericho', the single mast of a whale catcher, complete with crow's nest, emerges from the water. Between the buildings you can catch glimpses of 'Pig Street', once a busy thoroughfare in the summer months of the 1950s when over 300 station workers were on site – and just as many pigs, snuffling to and fro along the main 'drag' between the piggery at the head of Catcher Pier and the plan with its endless supply of tasty morsels.

Landings are possible on the beach to the south of the station. From here, a short walk inland across the football pitch leads to the cemetery and gentoo colony. The tussac covered headland of Hansen Point lies immediately south of the landing site and a visit to the World War II four-inch gun that sits atop the headland is well worth the scramble through tussac and elephant seal wallows.

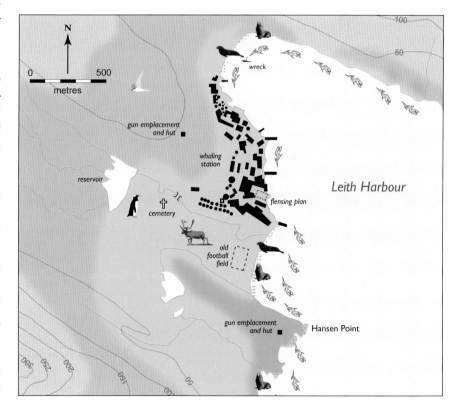

Life at Leith Harbour

Extracts from 'Shetland's Whalers Remember…' In 2001 Gibbie Fraser transcribed oral accounts from his Shetland whaling friends, providing us with one of the few descriptions of whaling that comes straight from the whalers themselves.

I got a job at the whaling a few weeks after the war started in September 1939. Addie Manson went all around getting as many men as he could. We joined the *Coronda*. She was loaded with coal for South Georgia. There must have been more than one hundred Shetlanders on her and there were a few Norwegians – more or less the Skippers of the whale catchers and the Mates and the gunners. (Peter Pole)

I had been [at Leith Harbour] a few days and was put on a job as a kettle emptier – the big tanks where the meat from the whales was put in to be boiled and the oil taken off after all the meat was cooked. There was a line of tanks on a railway with iron trolleys and wagons on them. They could carry a whole cartload of meat. When the meat was cooked in the tanks you opened the door and raked it into your wagon. When we got a full load on we pushed the wagon along the rails to the tip and we had to hook each one together and heave them up into the loft, into what they called the Chamber of Horror. You could not see the men down below for the steam off the hot meat and bones which were all ground and put through the mill. It came out at the other end and was bagged and weighed into hundred weight sacks and stored up in the very far end of the stone called the Guano Shed. (Peter Pole)

O ne day when there were no kettles to empty, the nine kettle emptiers out of the bone cookery and the three out of the meat cookery went in a whale catcher to the rookery [at Hercules Bay] where all the penguins were and gathered eggs for the whole day. We gathered many thousands of

eggs and that showed the number of penguins. I know I had quite a few in my pocket that night when we got back to Leith Harbour. It was one of the hardest days I had in South Georgia. The penguins were pecking at your legs and you had rubber boots on in a sunny day. It was a hot job carrying the buckets of eggs down to the whale boat and up the hill again among the penguins. (Peter Pole)

M any days when our watch was over we went out. We had bought skis and ski boots – and that was proper hilarity. Jimmy Harley and I were out skiing lots of days. We went up the side of Coronda Peak one day. It was frosty and we came down the valley

and up the other side but, not knowing that there was a deep drift of snow in the middle. I crashed into it going at quite a speed and nearly broke my neck. (Peter Pole)

W e used to swipe yeast from the baker to make home brew and we used to put God knows what all into a five gallon drum out in the locker and leave it for a while to ferment. But it tasted all right. During the winter we would make a brew and then put it through a still to get pure alcohol. It worked that you got a bottle of still from a gallon of home brew. Every now and again during the process, we had to take a little drop in a saucer and set match to it and if it lit up it would be all right but if it did not then it was poisonous. There was a hatch in the toilet that you opened and went down a short ladder to where the still was kept. Only the few who used it knew it was there. Willie Spence who was a Skipper came in every Saturday and he always tried to find the still. He stood many a time on top of the hatch and he would say, "Boys, I know there is something going on and if I can just find out". But he never did. (Nicol Thomson)

*T*he first winter I did there was very little mail but you could send a telegram home and get a reply back for about £2.00 so we used to do that regularly. The food was mostly Norwegian and some didn't like it but I thought the food was ok. (Willie Mail)

*T*here was a crowd of men on the island at the time but they all seemed to work well together and there was very little trouble. There was a picture house in Leith Harbour so we had pictures about three times a week during the winter and nearly everyone was making something – penguins out of whales teeth, trout nets out of old nylon rope and lots of other things so it helped to pass the time away during the long winter nights. (Willie Mail)

Left Scrimshaw; the sealer *Daisy* arriving at South Georgia in 1912

*S*ome days were very rough. The gales were well over one hundred miles per hour with severe blizzards that the mess boys carrying trays of food from the cookhouse had to dig a tunnel under the snow and they could walk to their full height carrying the trays of food into the mess room. (Peter Pole)

*T*here was no doubt about it; the whaling was a good way of life for us young fellows at the time. Now there is plenty of work in Shetland and at least it gives the poor old whale a chance to survive and that's certainly a good thing. I think most ex-whalers would say that they would go to the whaling again if they did not have to shoot the whales and I think that is probably true. (John Inkster)

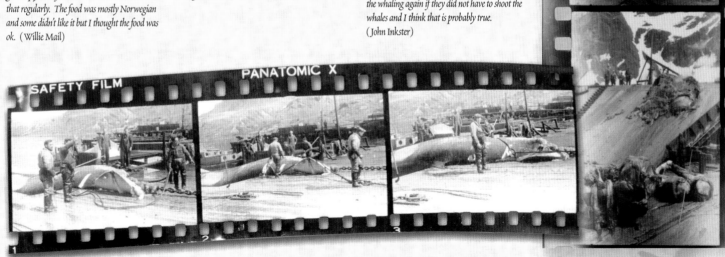

Shackleton Walk

FEATURES

▶ Retrace the route of Shackleton, Crean and Worsley

▶ Experience South Georgia's mountainous interior

▶ 'Crean Lake'

▶ 'Shackleton Waterfall'

▶ Views over Fortuna Bay and Stromness Bay

POINTERS

▶ Good visibility is essential

▶ A reasonable to good level of fitness is required

▶ Be prepared to traverse steep, sometimes unstable scree slopes

▶ Avoid areas of diving petrel burrows on scree slopes

▶ Once above the coastal vegetation, keep to scree and rock substrates, particularly on stream margins and adjacent to the waterfall

▶ Avoid walking on the moss beds alongside streams

LOCATION AND MAIN FEATURES

The 5·5 km long Shackleton Walk traverses the barren fellfield country between Fortuna Bay and Stromness Harbour. The route most commonly taken is an unmarked trail that starts in Fortuna Bay. From the beach, a steep uphill climb leads to a 300 m high pass and an even steeper descent into Shackleton Valley, finishing at the beach in Stromness Harbour near the whaling station. This is the same route taken by Shackleton, Crean and Worsley on the final leg of their 36 hour crossing of South Georgia, and hikers are rewarded with spectacular bird's-eye views of the island's mountains and glaciers.

See Stromness Harbour (page 98) and Fortuna Bay (page 78) for additional information.

LANDFORM AND HABITAT

The landscape of the Fortuna Bay and Stromness Bay area is quite distinctive, with well-developed scree slopes and conspicuous folding of the rocks which are typical of the Cumberland Bay Formation sedimentary sandstones and shales. There are few lovelier places for visitors to appreciate these landforms and habitat than the upper reaches of the Shackleton Walk above Fortuna Bay: brown textured scree slopes contrast with the green coastal tussac below and crisp white snow and ice fields above; the grey, debris-covered König Glacier colours the silt-laden waters of the bay a milky-blue. On a clear day, the hanging glaciers and ice cornices of the Allardyce Range create an alpine décor of exceptional beauty.

View of Stromness Bay and Shackleton Valley from the pass on the Shackleton Walk

The coastal vegetation at the start of the hike consists of a narrow fringe of tussac just above the gravel landing beach in the southeast corner of the bay. Further uphill, the tussac merges with *Festuca* grassland traversed here and there by mossy seepage gullies, and finally scree and rock with a scattering of occasional moss patches. Two prominent scree ridges separated by a stream extend inland and uphill from the beach in a southeasterly direction towards 'Crean Lake'. This tarn is a conspicuous landmark lying about midway to the saddle, and in early summer may still be partially covered by a fragile layer of slushy snow and ice.

The pass lies at 300 m altitude and is the highest point on the walk. Looking east from here, the views are dominated by huge zig-zag folds that trace a giant's scrawl across the face of the coastal cliffs

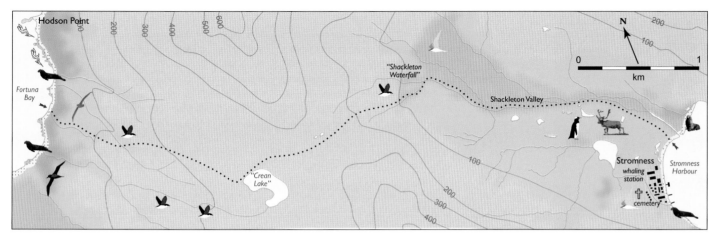

Hodson Point

Fortuna
Bay

"Shackleton
Waterfall"

Shackleton Valley

"Crean
Lake"

Stromness
whaling
station

Stromness
Harbour

cemetery

N

0   km   1

The view across an ice-covered 'Crean Lake' towards the König Glacier and the interior

95

of Busen Point. The whaling station of Stromness at the far end of the valley looks like a model village. At this altitude, the landscape is lunar. Jagged knife-edge outcrops of slate at the pass and a scattering of lichen-encrusted rocks and scree fragments, often arranged in regular geometric patterns by the annual freeze-thaw cycle, create a barren fellfield habitat which may be covered in snow even as late as December.

Scree, fellfield and rock outcrops extend all the way down from the pass into Shackleton Valley to meet the *Festuca* grassland and mire and bog communities on the lower slopes of the valley floor. Meltwater streams flow seaward into Stromness Harbour via several gullies and gorges, cascading over rock outcrops as waterfalls. The most conspicuous of these is the waterfall on the southern side of the head of Shackleton Valley, known as the 'Shackleton Waterfall'.

WILDLIFE

The landing beach in Fortuna Bay is occupied in season by breeding elephant seals and fur seals and several southern giant petrels nest in the *Festuca* above. South Georgia diving petrel burrows dot the scree slopes inland and there is also a small colony above the 'Shackleton Waterfall'. Reindeer graze both the Fortuna Bay area and Shackleton Valley. On the final section of the walk in Shackleton Valley a colony of gentoo penguins occupies the hillocky area on the south side of the river and fur seals dominate the beach area at Stromness.

HUMAN HISTORY

The story of Shackleton's remarkable crossing and epic journey inspires increasing numbers of visitors to retrace those legendary footsteps from Fortuna Bay to Stromness Harbour. Warmly dressed, well fed and watered, today's explorers present a stark contrast to the three scarecrow figures who struggled up the slope on the morning of 20th May 1916. Earlier that day, Shackleton, Crean and Worsley arrived at a col on Breakwind Ridge on the western shore of Fortuna Bay, having set off from King Haakon Bay some 26 hours previously. From their vantage point, some 600 m above the sea, the familiar, zig-zag folds in the cliffs of Busen Point were visible through the Stromness pass into the bay beyond. Final confirmation of their position came an hour later, when the blast of a steam whistle echoed over the mountains, the daily signal for whalers to turn-to for their day's work in the whaling station. Taking the most direct route to the beach below, Shackleton was lowered on a rope to hack steps in the ice-slope using an adze as an ice axe. It must have been such a relief to be at sea level again, to walk the beach from Whistle Cove to the far eastern shore with only a few seals and melt water streams to negotiate instead of crevasses and ice-covered cliff faces. The last uphill climb to the pass above Stromness was not without its adventures however, when the unsuspecting Crean broke through a layer of snow and ice to plunge waist-deep into the icy waters of 'Crean Lake'.

By early afternoon they were at the pass, and in Worsley's words looked *'down on to Stromness Bay, with two whalers steaming across it, looking like tiny insects on the water'*. Shackleton recalled that *'Minute figures walked to and fro caught our gaze, and then we saw the sheds and factory of Stromness whaling station. Once more we paused and shook one another warmly by the hand'*. One final hurdle lay before them however. In their exhausted state, the steep descent to the valley below presented a dilemma. Worsley would have opted for the steep scree gully, but Shackleton, not wanting to risk a downhill slide on ice and snow, chose to follow a nearby watercourse. And so they tramped downhill, knee-deep in icy water until brought to a halt by a 15 m waterfall encased in vertical cliff. Using the rope again to lower themselves, they finally reached the valley floor and wearily marched the final 2 km to the station. *'Ragged, filthy and evil-smelling'* they finally arrived on the doorstep of the manager's villa, making their first contact with the rest of the world in over 17 months.

VISITING THE SITE

Offering a geographical taste of the interior of the island and an historical perspective on South Georgia's most famous explorer, the Shackleton Walk is not for the faint-hearted. The steep scree slope descent to Shackleton Valley can test both nerves and knees if a snow-slope slide is not an option, and the steady climb up to the 300 m high mountain pass can present a taxing change to the comforts of life aboard a yacht or cruise ship. Sudden weather changes at this altitude should always be borne in mind. Always keep an eye on the weather, and look out for tell-tale signs of strong winds and the formation of mist or low cloud.

As with all sites at South Georgia, once you leave the coastal fringe behind, both vegetation and wildlife thin out considerably. However, there are southern giant petrels above the landing beach at Fortuna Bay and small numbers of South Georgia diving petrels burrow in fine scree. Wilson's storm-petrels are also found in boulder screes, so take care not to dislodge rocks, and avoid areas with burrows, mosses and lichens when walking on the inland fellfield country. In the area of 'Shackleton Waterfall', choose a route over scree and rock in preference to the grass-covered slope adjacent to the waterfall.

Right Moss banks thrive on the slopes behind the whaling station
Below Reindeer make their way down the ridge from 'Crean Lake' towards Fortuna Bay

Facing page The 'Shackleton Waterfall'

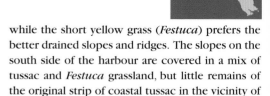

STROMNESS HARBOUR

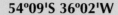

54°09'S 36°02'W

See Shackleton Walk for additional information and see page 95 for a map of Stromness.

FEATURES
▸ Historic site of Shackleton's arrival at end of his South Georgia crossing
▸ Whaling station
▸ Reindeer
▸ Fur seal pups

POINTERS
▸ Beware: dense fur seal breeding beach
▸ Walk up the valley can be wet underfoot, and early in the season may be covered in deep snow
▸ Keep 200m from whaling station
▸ Give gentoo penguins the right of way

LOCATION AND MAIN FEATURES

Stromness Harbour is situated in the central harbour of Stromness Bay. It was here that Shackleton finished his epic voyage, walking into the now derelict whaling station of Stromness which stands at the southern end of a long grey sand beach at the head of the harbour. This is an excellent site for reindeer, but it is the fur seal pups which gather in their hundreds near the mouth of the river in mid-summer that are the undisputed wildlife highlight.

Behind the station, Shackleton Valley extends inland and westward up to a pass leading over to Fortuna Bay. A picturesque waterfall situated at the head of the valley lies on the route most probably taken by Shackleton, and flows into the large swiftly-running river that joins the sea at the northern end of the beach.

LANDFORM AND HABITAT

Stromness Harbour and Shackleton Valley are contained in a huge U-shaped valley, flanked on either side by impressively steep brown scree slopes rising to 500m high mountain ridges. There are some excellent examples of glacial landform features on the south side of the river, notably moraine ridges, small tarns and rounded hummocks called roches moutonnes.

Mosses, rushes and other mire and bog plants cloak the valley floor in a patchwork of soft, wet swampy areas that are best avoided during a hike, while the short yellow grass (*Festuca*) prefers the better drained slopes and ridges. The slopes on the south side of the harbour are covered in a mix of tussac and *Festuca* grassland, but little remains of the original strip of coastal tussac in the vicinity of the whaling station

WILDLIFE

Starting in January when only a few weeks old, fur seal pups congregate in their hundreds near the river mouth, gambolling in the shallows, play fighting and waiting for a meal from their mothers who arrive at regular intervals between offshore feeding trips. Inquisitive by nature, they will investigate any visitor who stays still for long enough. Several hundred elephant seals also breed and moult here, seeming to enjoy the shelter of the derelict station buildings as much as their traditional wallows on the outskirts of the station.

Herds of reindeer are often seen grazing in Shackleton Valley and amongst the station buildings. There is a small gentoo penguin colony located among the hills between the whaling station and the river about 800m inland from the landing site. Skuas nest on the route between the beach and the penguins, some quite close to the track to the 'Shackleton Waterfall'. A few Antarctic terns nest on the gravel river bed in Shackleton Valley and there is a large colony situated on the slopes behind the whaling station.

HUMAN HISTORY

The whaling company Sandefjord Hvalfangerselskab started operations in Stromness Harbour in 1907. Whales were processed on board the floating factory ship *Fridtjof Nansen II* which was moored on the north side of the harbour about 1·5km from the whaling station. The ruins of a small dam and stone building are still visible there today, as are whale vertebrae strewn along the shoreline, reminders of the era when processing whales was a wasteful business.

Improvements came in 1912, when new Falkland Islands and Dependencies conservation regulations stipulated that the entire whale be processed, an operation that was not possible on board floating factories. The success of the land station was such that in 1913-14, Stromness produced as much oil from 442 whales as the floating factory ship had produced from 912 whales two years earlier.

This success lasted up until the 1930s when world market prices and whale stocks collapsed due to the ruthless efficiency of pelagic whaling operations. The impact on Stromness was huge: in the 1931–32 season, the station ceased processing whales and was subleased as a ship repair yard to the South

99

Georgia Company (Christian Salvesen & Co. Ltd.), which owned the neighbouring whaling station at Leith Harbour. Stromness finally closed in the 1960-61 season when the company ceased whaling at South Georgia.

VISITING THE SITE

Visitors have the choice of approaching Stromness from the sea or via the overland route from Fortuna Bay, known as the Shackleton Walk or Hike.

The most frequently used landing site is to the north of the station near the collection of whale catcher propellers - a legacy from the station's days as a ship repair yard. Nearby are two whale catcher masts and crow's nests. The propellers are almost exactly 200 m from the station buildings and provide a useful boundary marker to the Government's station exclusion zone, which is indicated by a large conspicuous sign close to the landing site. The area around the station is further cordoned off by numerous elephant seal wallows.

The most popular walking route is up Shackleton Valley to the 'Shackleton Waterfall', a 4 km round trip along the course of the braided river. Rubber boots are useful as it is very wet underfoot. Take care that your route does not cross the track used by the gentoo penguins walking to and from the sea, and be prepared for large numbers of fur seals.

Top Williwaws whip up the sea in front of Stromness whaling station
Bottom The characteristic zig-zag foilds of the cliffs at Busen Point

Top (right to left) Fur seal pup; Adder's tongue fern; Liverwort *Marchantia* sp.
Below View of Stromness whaling station from Shackleton valley looking across to Jason Peak

HUSVIK

LOCATION AND MAIN FEATURES

The whaling station is situated at the northern end of a long sandy beach at the head of Husvik Harbour, southernmost of the three harbours in Stromness Bay. On the southern outskirts of the station and beyond the 200 m exclusion zone are the station manager's villa (the long white bungalow) and the grey corrugated iron-clad 'radio shack', both used regularly as base camps by scientific and expedition field parties. Between these two buildings, mounted on a pedestal, sits a harpoon gun, a monument to times past. South of the station, is a cemetery containing some 37 graves marking the last resting place of Norwegian whalers. Reindeer thrive on the sheltered grassy slopes and valleys around the harbour. Large numbers of elephant seals haul out to breed and moult on the sandy beach infront of the station, competing with the growing population of fur seals.

LANDFORM AND HABITAT

Entered between Tonsberg Point to the north and Kelp Point on its southern shore, the inner part of Husvik Harbour is protected to seaward by Bar Rocks and extensive kelp beds running from Kanin Point across to Point Purvis.

The landscape around Husvik is dominated by two major drainage systems, one channeled from the north through Karrakatta Valley and the other cascading down the steep gorges of Husdal to the west. Winding their way between moraine ridges,

steep-sided cliffs and scree slopes, the rivers spill out onto the large fluvio-glacial plain on which the station was built. The northern river passes directly through the station and enters the sea next to the jetty, while the Husdal waters breach the shingle beach to the south of the manager's villa. In periods of heavy rain, the entire area around the buildings may be underwater. Many small lakes have formed in the hollows amongst the glacial deposits, and Karrakatta Valley in particular is dotted with a series of pools and lakes all the way up to the saddle that leads over to Fortuna Bay.

The hinterland surrounding the station contains a diverse range of plant communities, from coastal tussac to high altitude fellfield but dominated principally by *Festuca* grassland on the well-drained slopes and by rushes and mosses in the wetter areas, with peat beds up to 2 m deep in places. Introduced plants are abundant, among them dandelions, chickweed, St Johns-wort, yarrow and even cowberries. However, the burnet and lichens that would normally flourish in the *Festuca* are much sought after by reindeer, and in heavily grazed areas have been replaced by mosses and the introduced annual meadow-grass which colours some of the coastal hills a distinctive bright green, particularly near any gentoo penguin colonies.

One of South Georgia's most unusual glaciated landscape features is Gulbrandsen Lake, hidden away in the mountains above Husdal at the edge of the Neumayer Glacier. Here meltwater fills a valley

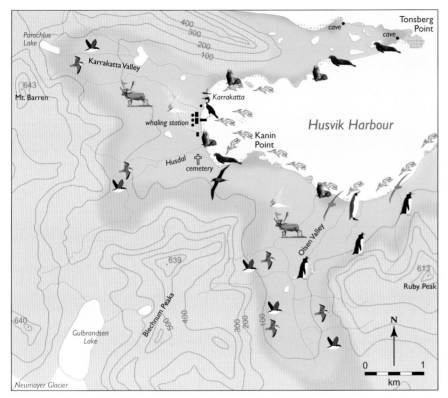

Parochlus Lake

400
300
200
100

Karrakatta Valley

643
Mt. Barren

Karrakatta

whaling station

Husdal
cemetery

Kanin
Point

Husvik Harbour

cave

cave

Tonsberg
Point

639

Blechnum Peaks

Olsen Valley

613
Ruby Peak

640

Gulbrandsen
Lake

500
400
300
200
100

N

0   1
km

Neumayer Glacier

Top Husvik whaling station manager's villa
Bottom Small fern *Blechnum penna-marina*

dammed on one side by the glacier as it flows past on its way to Cumberland West Bay. Chunks of calved ice float on the still waters of the lake, although some summers the water may drain away, literally in a matter of days, leaving ice stranded on the barren floor of the empty basin, slowly melting and sculpted by wind and sun. The walls of the empty basin are marked by prominent terraces which form a series of concentric lines, indicating former lake levels.

WILDLIFE

Reindeer, elephant seals and fur seals dominate the wildlife at Husvik and intermingle on the grassy flats behind the beaches. Fur seals were first recorded breeding in Stromness Bay in the late 1980s, and have increased beyond all expectations. In January 2004, researchers from the Sea Mammal Research Unit working from Husvik counted 21,000 fur seal pups along approximately 11 km of coastline between Husvik Harbour and Stromness whaling station. They also initiated an elephant seal research project designed to measure oceanographic characteristics (temperature and salinity in particular) of the seals' foraging areas, through the use of satellite relayed data loggers attached to the seals (see page 116).

Between 800 and 1000 reindeer graze the lowland coastal areas from Cumberland West Bay to Fortuna Bay. Known as the Busen herd, they are descendants of three males and four females introduced by the Norwegians in 1925. Olsen Valley on the south shore of Husvik Harbour is one of their favourite grazing areas and females gather here in their hundreds in spring to give birth to wobbly-legged fawn-coloured

calves. On the inland slopes of this valley and in the upper reaches of Husdal and Karrakatta Valley, well beyond the rat-infested coastal tussac, are scattered colonies of Antarctic prions and South Georgia diving petrels, their oval-shaped burrow entrances conspicuously pock-marking the scree slopes.

Closer to the station, a large colony of very noisy and aggressive terns usually occupies the gravel river bed behind the station, while the jetty, complete with narrow gauge railway, has proved to be a popular nesting site for a small colony of blue-eyed shags that raise their young on the very end of the rickety wooden decking alongside a pair of kelp gulls.

HUMAN HISTORY

The elephant seal beaches around Husvik Harbour were well known to early sealers, and remnants of huts are discernible at Kanin Point and Tonsberg Point. Whaling began at the site in 1907 with the arrival of a floating factory ship *Bucentaur*, followed by the construction of a shore station in 1910. Today the station still retains an air of temporary abandon rather than total dereliction. A prominent bluff at the north end of the main beach dominates the flensing plan and slipway where the 32 m long steel-riveted vessel *Karrakatta* sits high and dry, remarkably intact and a distinctive feature on the shoreline. Built in Christiana (now Oslo) in 1912 for an Australian whaling company, she once worked out of Stewart Island in New Zealand as a whale catcher before ending up at Husvik in her present position for use as a boiler: a hole was cut in her starboard side to provide easy access to the boiler room where a coal-fired boiler produced quantities of steam which was piped to the nearby steam-powered engineering workshop.

During the heyday of whaling, Husvik was one of the most productive and profitable of all the whaling stations, producing more barrels per whale than any other. Operations continued until 1931 when world whale oil prices collapsed due to overproduction as a result of the growth of pelagic whaling, and the station closed, eventually re-opening at the end of World War II when oil prices rose once again. In the late 1950s the company invested in the construction of a meat freezing plant, despite the growing scarcity of whales. It was operational for one season only, 1959–60, and the following year was dismantled and moved to Grytviken, and the station closed permanently after more than 40 years of operation.

VISITING THE SITE

Landings on the beach south of the station are possible in most conditions and from here it is a short walk to the cemetery and manager's villa. Longer hikes up Husdal to Gulbrandsen Lake or south along the coast to Olsen Valley and inland across to Carlita Bay in Cumberland West Bay are good half day trips which require careful planning, but are well worth the effort. Waterproof footwear is advisable, as not only is the ground boggy in places, but there are several streams to be crossed. An offshore zodiac cruise along the waterfront can be equally rewarding as it affords good views of the jetty and buildings, *Karrakatta* and engineering workshops, and the antics of the fur and elephant seals amongst the kelp.

JASON HARBOUR

54°11'S 36° 30'W

Named after C. A. Larsen's whaling vessel Jason *which anchored in the bay in April 1894.*

FEATURES
▸ Hut
▸ Small king penguin colony
▸ Elephant seal wallows

POINTERS
▸ Avoid getting too close to the breeding king penguins
▸ Take care when walking around the pools
▸ Be sure to close the hut door when leaving

LOCATION AND MAIN FEATURES

Jason Harbour lies on the northwestern shore of Cumberland West Bay between Tor Point and West Point. It affords good anchorage in northerly winds although prevailing winds may occasionally fill the harbour with ice from the Neumayer Glacier. A low isthmus separates the anchorage from Little Jason Lagoon, where a shallow rock-strewn entrance leads to an inner land-locked lagoon over 500m wide, nestled at the foot of Jason Peak. Large numbers of elephant seals breed on the main beach and in recent years, fur seals have taken over the western end in the vicinity of the little red hut.

LANDFORM AND HABITAT

Much of the Cumberland Bay shoreline has been sculptured by cirque glaciers at sea level, resulting in the formation of circular bays such as Jason Harbour. Examples of the various processes of glacial erosion are plentiful in the area: inland from the hut is a level outwash plain backed by a 10–15m high raised beach; the remains of a moraine form the low isthmus that separates Jason Lagoon from the harbour; 15–20m high roches moutonnées can be seen between Hut Point and Lagoon Point.

Vegetation in the area is sparse since virtually all coastal tussac has been severely over-grazed by reindeer. The resulting network of interconnecting pools, streams and elephant seal wallows behind the beach is a wasteland of closely-cropped grasses and rounded moss-covered hummocks.

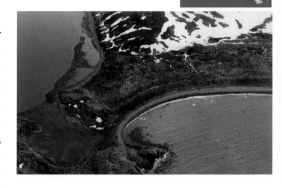

WILDLIFE

Jason Harbour has a surprising diversity of wildlife. There is a small king penguin colony of about 30 pairs inland from the main beach among the pools, an unusual choice of habitat for kings. Nesting in the *Festuca* on the top of the nearby raised beach slope, is a pair of skuas. Their nest is surrounded by a scattering of bones – the remains of South Georgia diving petrels which burrow into nearby inland scree slopes and provide the skuas with a regular source of food.

Fur seals began breeding here in about 2000, and their numbers increase annually, as do the non-breeders which haul out in the tussac by the hut. During the spring, the main beach is occupied by several large elephant seal harems, and the wallows at the back of the beach are popular moulting areas later in the season. Elephant seal pups and weaners occasionally get into difficulties in the deep pools of mud and water, becoming trapped in the slippery steep-sided hollows, and eventually starving to death. Pintail are often seen feeding around the wallows and along the foreshore at low tide, and kelp gulls and blue-eyed shags nest in small numbers along the cliffs between Hut Point and Lagoon Point.

HUMAN HISTORY

The harbour was first charted in 1894 by Captain C.A. Larsen aboard *Jason*, in company with *Hertha* and *Castor*. The vessels spent nearly three months at South Georgia exploring much of the northern coastline including Larsen Harbour, Royal Bay and Cumberland Bay. Larsen visited Jason Harbour again in April 1902 as commander of the Swedish South Polar Expedition vessel *Antarctic,* taking scientists to a number of sites around the island. In 1909 Larsen was granted a 15 year lease of land at Jason Harbour, five years after establishing Grytviken whaling station. The lease also included provision for a whaling licence for two whale catchers but there was never any intention to establish a whaling station on the site. Instead, a small refuge hut was built in 1911, and it still stands today.

VISITING THE SITE

The most sheltered landing site is at the west end of the shingle beach close to the hut. It is also a favourite with fur seals so take care on landing. Inside the hut is an old wooden table which has acted as a visitor's book for crew

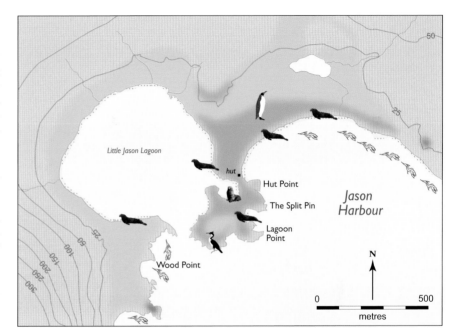

from several whaling, government and research vessels. The earliest distinguishable name carved into the wooden table is that of *Meteor* (1926). A small coal burning stove stands in the corner, its chimney set at a jaunty angle where it emerges from the roof. From the hut, and taking care to avoid any elephant seals immersed in wallows, it is possible to find a path through the maze of pools in the direction of the king penguin colony, and from there, loop back along the cobbled beach to the landing site.

GRYTVIKEN AND KING EDWARD POINT

54° 15'S 36° 45'W

Grytviken ('pot cove' in both Norwegian and Swedish) was named after sealers' trypots found at the site. King Edward Point was named for King Edward VII.

FEATURES

- ▸ Historic seat of government administration
- ▸ Grytviken whaling station
- ▸ South Georgia museum and gift shop
- ▸ British Antarctic Survey research station
- ▸ Shackleton's grave and memorial cross
- ▸ Church and cemetery, Discovery House and Post Office

POINTERS

- ▸ For cruise ships: no more than 100 people in the church, cemetery or museum at any time
- ▸ Respect and do not walk over graves in the cemetery
- ▸ With the exception of the Post Office, do not enter buildings at King Edward Point unless invited to do so
- ▸ Keep a safe distance from the elephant and fur seals, especially near the cemetery
- ▸ Be alert for ordnance hazards when walking in the area
- ▸ Minimise use of vessel lights at night to prevent bird strike

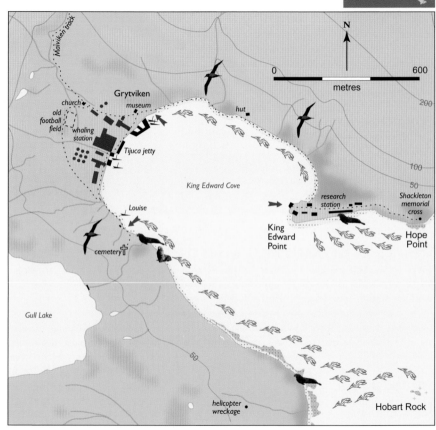

LOCATION AND MAIN FEATURES

Grytviken and King Edward Point lie within King Edward Cove, a sheltered harbour tucked between Hope Point and Hobart Rock on the western shore of Cumberland East Bay. The rusting ruins of the Grytviken whaling station are situated on a level plain at the head of the cove, backed by steep hills and mountains. Now the site of the South Georgia Museum, the station remains a focal point of interest for many visitors, as does Sir Ernest Shackleton's grave in the nearby whalers' cemetery, and his memorial cross on Hope Point at the eastern entrance to the cove. King Edward Point, a low promontory just below Hope Point, is the site of the South Georgia Government's administrative centre and fisheries research facility.

The scenery in this area is exceptionally beautiful even by South Georgia standards: the glaciers and snow covered peaks of the Allardyce Range – Mt. Sugartop, Mt. Paget, Mt. Roots, Nordenskjold Peak, Mt. Kling and Mt. Brooker – form a magnificent backdrop to the cove, and the views from King Edward Point in particular, must be among the finest on earth.

LANDFORM AND HABITAT

Grytviken is virtually encircled by a rampart of steep-walled mountains, with the dramatic peaks of Mt. Duse (507 m) and Mt. Hodges (633 m) casting long shadows over the two settlements for three months

Right Grytviken church was originally from Strømmen in Norway, and was dismantled and brought to Grytviken in 1913. Several weddings have taken place here in recent years.

of every winter. Their rock faces are constantly freezing, thawing and fracturing to form the coarse, sharp screes that characterise the lower slopes. The area has the reputation of enjoying a better climate than the rest of the island but even so, katabatic winds of hurricane force may occasionally sweep across the bay, whipping the water into walls of spray and suspending small boat operations.

At the height of summer, there is a green luxuriance to the vegetation around Grytviken and an abundance of burnet and lichens. The steep coastal slopes along the southern shore of the cove are covered in continuous stands of tussac and burnet. From the top of the slope, a vast expanse of *Festuca* grassland with a thick understorey of lichens and mosses extends around Gull Lake over gently undulating terrain to meet the scree slopes on Brown Mountain. Bogs and mires fill the depressions and valleys; burnet carpets the lower margins of scree slopes, thinning out to a scattering of grasses, with lichens and mosses on the more exposed knolls and hill crests. Patches of introduced plants such as dandelions, chickweed, sheep sorrel and various grasses of European origin, notably the annual meadow-grass, thrive in the vicinity of the whaling station and cemetery.

WILDLIFE

Elephant seals, and increasingly fur seals, occupy the main beaches around the bay. Each spring about 150 female elephant seals haul out on the long gravel beach next to the buildings at King Edward Point and attendant bulls often wake the human residents with their jealous roars and the occasional bloody battle as aspiring beachmasters attempt to move in. By December, the black-coated newborn pups have moulted into fat, silver-coated weaners that gather in little bathing parties by the boatshed, sniffing their way curiously around the jetty, testing the water. Large numbers of king penguins come ashore to moult during the summer months. They stand in silent groups around the shore, shedding feathers patiently and scarcely moving.

South Georgia pintail and Norway rats scurry about in the tussac that covers much of the Point and small numbers of white-chinned petrels and the occasional light-mantled sooty albatross nest on the tussac slopes above. Kelp gulls are common in the harbour, their moss and limpet-lined nests most often found on low rock outcrops along the shore, and a dozen or so pairs nest colonially amongst the burnet and on the shores of Gull Lake. Antarctic terns also nest in this area. A small flock of speckled teal occasionally visit the cove in the winter months. They resemble the native pintail, and are thought to be descendants of storm-blown birds from the Falklands.

HUMAN HISTORY

Grytviken has been the centre of human activity on the island since 1904, when C.A. Larsen established the island's first whaling station on the level land at the head of the cove. Larsen first visited the area in 1902 when he was captain of Nordenskjold's expedition vessel *Antarctic* (see page 34). J. Gunnar Andersson, the expedition's chief scientist, discovered the cove while exploring the area from his campsite at Maiviken. He found evidence of early sealing activities: at King Edward Point: a 10m long green-painted wooden boat or shallop (now lying beneath the jetty as part of the foundations) and seven trypots, two of which are displayed outside the South Georgia Museum.

Antarctic was anchored for a month at Grytviken while the expedition conducted detailed studies of the geology, plants and wildlife. With its sheltered harbour and plentiful supply of freshwater, Grytviken was the pick of sites for what was to be the first whaling station in Antarctic waters. In November 1904, Larsen returned to South Georgia, having raised sufficient capital in Argentina to form the whaling company Compania Argentina de Pesca. A brand-new steam whale catcher *Fortuna* and two transport vessels *Louise* and *Rolf* sailed from Sandefjord, carrying a cargo of prefabricated wooden buildings and factory equipment. Less than one month after arriving at South Georgia, a slipway, three buildings and factory with 12 cookers were ready for use, and on 22nd December 1904, the first whale was being flensed on the plan. Over the years the whaling station grew to house about 300 men and processed more than 54,000 whales, before its final closure on 4th December 1964, after six decades of operations. A Norwegian caretaker, Ragnor Thorsen, remained at the station until 1971, after which it was abandoned to the rigours of weather and looting sprees by passing visitors.

In 1979, Christian Salvesen & Co. Ltd. acquired the Grytviken lease (having already acquired those for Prince Olav, Leith Harbour, Husvik and Stromness)

and in 1990–91 the company joined forces with the British Foreign and Commonwealth Office to fund a partial clean-up of the stations. Following this, on 27th February 1992, all leases reverted to the South Georgia Government. However, it was not until 2005, after a two-year remedial operation funded by the Government of South Georgia, that the station was declared safe for visitors. Enormous quantities of hazardous waste were removed and many of the buildings and the entire flensing plan area were demolished. Future projects include repairs to the Tijuca jetty to facilitate passenger landings and berth for yachts.

VISITING GRYTVIKEN
by Tim and Pauline Carr

The South Georgia Museum at Grytviken was established in 1992 by Nigel Bonner, an ex-sealing inspector from the whaling days and a world renowned expert on whales and seals. After retiring from his post as deputy director of the British Antarctic Survey in 1987, Nigel and a small dedicated team undertook the task of renovating the long-abandoned manager's villa in the whaling station at Grytviken. Today, under the auspices of the South Georgia Government and Museum Trust, the museum, church and cemetery undergo an annual repair and improvement programme that ensures the complex is maintained as a high-quality visitor centre.

Right The small library in a room at the back of the church (*top*); Shackleton was buried in the Grytviken cemetery in 1922 (*bottom*)

Facing page The South Georgia museum from the bow of the sealer *Dias*

111

exhibits housed in a total of eight rooms in the smartly painted red and white villa. The Bonner Room contains general information for visitors as well as a selection of maritime history. Highlights of discovery of the island and Shackleton's expeditions are on display in the Fullerton Room. Activities from 18th and 19th century sealing and 20th century whaling are shown in the Larsen Room. The three Whalers' Trades Rooms explain the self-sufficiency of the whaling stations, displaying tools and equipment of the tradesmen; while the living conditions of whalers in the 1950s are shown in the Ringdal Room where a bunkroom from the whalers' barracks has been reconstructed. Displays in the Allardyce Room show scenes of modern whaling, from the chase, to the flensing plan, to the end products. Plants, animals, fish and other aspects of the island's natural history are on display in the Prince Room. Finally, exhibits in the Jarvis Room portray the development of the island's administration and government, with mention of the events of 1982 when Argentina invaded South Georgia.

Judging from the comments of visitors, the displays more than amply fulfil expectations and the little shop with its selection of books, clothing, postcards and jewellery has proved very popular. Stamps can also be bought here and there is a Royal Mail post box at the entrance. Credit cards are welcome, and all sales provide essential income for the running of the museum and associated workshops, storerooms, library, archives, curators' residence and summer staff.

The easiest beaches for small boat landings at Grytviken are directly in front of the museum next to the sealing vessels *Albatros* and *Dias*, and in front of the cemetery near *Louise*. The museum and gift shop are housed in the former whaling station manager's villa less than 100 m from the landing beach.

Since its beginnings, the museum has developed from a mainly whaling-orientated exhibition of memorabilia from bygone days into a well-equipped visitor's centre that portrays the story of the island, its history and natural environment in a series of

The whalers' church is only a few minutes walk from the museum. Prefabricated in Norway for C. A. Larsen, it was consecrated on Christmas Day 1913 and the two bells which were first rung at midnight on that Christmas Eve still hang in the steeple today. At the back of the church is a small library containing books in English and Norwegian, originally from Grytviken whaling station library and some of the Stromness Bay whaling stations.

The whalers' cemetery, situated on the south shore of the bay and enclosed by a white fence, contains a total of 64 graves, including those of Sir Ernest Shackleton and Felix Artuso, an Argentine submariner who died during the re-taking of South Georgia in 1982. The earliest marked grave dates back to 1846 when a typhus outbreak on board a British sealing vessel *Esther* claimed the lives of five of her crew.

There are many enjoyable walks in the vicinity of Grytviken and regardless of which hill you climb, each ascent gives spectacular views of Cumberland Bay and the Allardyce Range beyond. Gull Lake is on the south shore of the cove and a short distance from the station. This artificial body of water was created in 1912 after a dam was built on the ridge above the cemetery, providing hydro-electric power to the whaling station for nearly 60 years. A gradual traverse along the hillside above the cemetery, and past the two remnant wooden stumps of the compass-aligning markers erected by men of Shackleton's *Endurance* in 1914, leads to the remains of an Argentine helicopter shot down in 1982. Be aware that there may be objects and unexploded ordnance dating from the 1982 conflict

and subsequent military occupation of the area: if you find anything that looks suspicious, record its position and notify the Government Officer.

Walks in the area to the north of the station lead to other magnificent lookouts on the lower slopes of Mt. Duse. Climbing further inland, the keen hiker may be tempted to explore Bore Valley and walk over to Maiviken (see page 118). And of course, the track to King Edward Point around the shores of the cove is a regularly trodden route for visitors and residents alike. It is also the only vehicular road on the island although traffic is fairly quiet, except for the occasional fur seal suddenly emerging from the tussac at head-height close to the track at 'Ambush Corner'.

Below Residents of King Edward Point and cruise ship passengers alike celebrate Christmas Day each year in the festively decorated church

VISITING KING EDWARD POINT
by Sarah Lurcock

King Edward Point is home to most of the island's small resident population. Visitors may walk through the research station to Shackleton's memorial cross on Hope Point and call in at the Post Office. If arriving by small boat, visitors may land at the jetty where several vessels are usually moored, notably the research station's launches.

The track takes you past Discovery House, where a whaling harpoon gun and maritime memorabilia are on display outside. Built in 1925, this building was the residence and laboratory for the *Discovery* Investigations personnel (see page 38). Next door is the Government Officer's residence, Carse House, built in 2005. The long low modern building that stretches the length of the foreshore is the government's fisheries research facility run by the British Antarctic Survey (BAS) (see page 48). It also houses the offices of the Government Officer and the Post Office where stamps, postcards, First Day Covers and commemorative coins are available. Adjoining this is Everson House, the main living quarters for BAS personnel who spend up to two years at the station. Medical facilities include a well-equipped medical centre in nearby Larsen House, and a resident doctor is present to provide cover for the fishing fleet, as well as residents.

Opposite Everson House is the oldest surviving building on the Point, the customs warehouse and gaol, built in 1914 and used more often to accommodate early expeditioners than prisoners. Allegedly the first inmate escaped before the building had been completed, and took off up the slope towards Mt. Duse, pelting his pursuers with rocks. After a cold night on the hill however, he returned voluntarily to imprisonment. The red container alongside the gaol is the sauna, a much appreciated luxury after the traditional mid-winter swim. At the end of the track on Hope Point stands Shackleton's memorial cross, and the views here of Grytviken and the Allardyce Range are superb.

Nacreous lenticular clouds over Cumberland Bay from King Edward Point (*above*); Shackleton memorial cross, erected by the crew of *Quest* at Hope Point in 1922 (*below*)

Facing page Path leading from King Edward Point to the cross at Hope Point (*left*); the cruise ship *Explorer II* off King Edward Point (*right*)

Southern elephant seals – a species of many extremes

Martin Biuw,
Sea Mammal
Research Unit

When most people think of elephant seals, the first image that springs to mind is usually that of huge, aggressive, ugly fighting beasts with drooping trunk-like noses and blood-covered chests and throats. While this is a spectacular and common sight during the short, intensive breeding period, it is only one of several unusual characteristics of these marine mammals. These are the largest living seal species (southern elephant seals being slightly larger than their northern counterparts), and have an impressive diving ability; spending 90% of their time submerged and attaining depths of about 1,800 m during dives that may last for up to two hours. For elephant seals there is a complete separation between feeding at sea and fasting on land during the two main haulout periods: breeding and moulting. Effectively they have had to adapt to extreme fluctuations in body reserves (fat and protein), and as such can survive several months on energy reserves, stored mainly in their blubber fat, accumulated while feeding at sea.

Besides their large size (mature males weighing up to 4·5 tonnes), there are extreme differences between the sexes of elephant seals. Males can be more than ten times the size of females and have a distinctly different appearance. Such 'sexual dimorphism' is common among species with a polygynous mating system, i.e. where individuals of one sex (usually males) can defend large numbers of the opposite sex with which they mate. Successful adult elephant seal males (harem masters) can hold harems of several hundred females, and their ability to defend these from other males during an extended period, whilst fasting, is highly dependent on their size, feeding success and fighting ability.

Sexually mature bulls start arriving at the breeding beaches around mid-August to compete for the best harem locations before the arrival of pregnant females, the first of which usually come ashore in early September. Females normally give birth within four to five days after arrival, and a female will usually give birth within two to three days of the same date in consecutive years. Pups nurse for three weeks on their mothers' fat and protein rich milk. The resources that make up this milk are derived entirely from the female's body reserves, and females lose about 30% of their body mass (mostly fat) during lactation.

At the end of lactation, females come into oestrus, and after they have mated (usually with her harem master, but sometimes with subordinate males as well) they depart to sea to replenish their exhausted body reserves before they return for the annual moult sometime around January–March.

When mothers go to sea, their pups are abandoned and remain on the beaches fasting for four to eight weeks. The reason for this extended fast is not clear, but since pups spend increasingly more time in the water as the fast goes on, it is likely that this "post-weaning fast" allows them to go through physiological changes to prepare them for diving and feeding at sea. When pups finally go to sea in late November – early January, they may travel more than 4,000 km from land to find food. Successful females may eventually return to breed for the first time aged three to four years, while surviving males may return as a challenger to the harem masters around age 10.

But perhaps the most impressive aspect of elephant seals is their physiological adaptations. Their extreme diving behaviour obviously places tremendous demands on the efficiency and capability of storing and conserving oxygen. Elephant seals have a high concentration of oxygen-binding haemoglobin in their blood, and their proportionately large blood volume serves as an important oxygen store as well as circulation system. This oxygen-storing capability is further increased by large quantities of oxygen-binding myoglobin in their muscle tissues. Their ability to remain submerged for long periods of time is further enhanced by other adaptations that allow elephant seals to reduce their oxygen use: for example, by effectively restricting the flow of blood to peripheral body parts, seals can conserve oxygen while maintaining blood flow to vital organs such as the brain and heart.

Over the past 10 years, information about migrations and diving behaviour of elephant seals has been collected using data logging instruments glued to their fur. In some cases, these data are relayed via satellite, allowing scientists to monitor the seals movements and behaviour in near real-time.

These instruments have revealed the astonishing diving behaviour of elephant seals, with seals regularly diving below 500 m for about 45 minutes or more. They have also shown that seals travel several thousand kilometres in search of food, and that individual seals often return to the same feeding grounds year after year. These new methods of following seals while at sea provide crucial information about important times and areas for feeding. While there are no known immediate threats to southern elephant seals, such information helps us better understand the potential interactions with commercial fishing and other human activities, as well as how these animals interact with their physical and biological environment.

Although there may be some small overlap at the edge of feeding boundaries, the elephant seals of the southern ocean can be divided into four distinct populations. Of these, the South Georgia elephant seal population comprises the largest (400,000 out of a total global population of 538,000 animals). While the population dynamics of the different stocks varies, it appears that the overall trend is stable.

Below male (*top*) and female elephant seals (*bottom*)

Facing page A young elephant seal weaner, with misplaced hope, cuddling up to a large male

MAIVIKEN

Meaning 'May Cove', the bay was named by the Swedish South Polar Expedition who landed here on 1st May 1902.

FEATURES
▸ Sealers cave
▸ Hike to Grytviken
▸ Freshwater lakes

POINTERS
▸ Dense breeding fur seal beach
▸ Flashlights recommended for visits to the cave
▸ Hikers should be prepared for boggy ground and some steep ascents and descents on rocky ground
▸ Stay on the track
▸ Avoid walking on moss beds
▸ Report any ordnance or suspect items to the Government Officer

LOCATION AND MAIN FEATURES

Maiviken is tucked into a coastline of cliff headlands and scree slopes that separates Cumberland East and West Bays. Entered between Rocky Point and Mai Point, the bay is encircled by steep-sided mountains and cliffs, with three small tussac-fringed coves on its eastern shore – Tortula Cove, Burnet Cove and Poa Cove. The area was well-known to early sealers, who have left traces of their presence in several of the caves around the bay. Fur seals and elephant seals breed here and there is a colony of gentoo penguins at Tortula Cove.

LANDFORM, CLIMATE AND HABITAT

The horseshoe-shaped indentation of Maiviken forms a sheltered suntrap where an exceptionally luxuriant and varied assemblage of plants has developed, particularly on the lake-studded undulating lowland area on the eastern side of the bay where dense tussac fringes the foreshore and margins of numerous streams, pools and lakes. The hills are covered with a mix of tussac, *Festuca*, burnet, mosses and lichens. Shield fern, brittle bladder fern and adder's tongue are not uncommon, and in the damper depressions are liverworts, Antarctic hairgrass and rushes. Above the lower lakes and at the top of the 40 m high sea cliffs is a grassy plateau and catchment area for a number of other lakes, including Maivatn. From here, the ground rises steeply to bare scree slopes and rocky bluffs in Bore Valley, a natural 'highway'

linking Maivken to Grytviken. Here, tussac and *Festuca* are replaced by a sparse scattering of grasses, mosses and lichens that is typical of the island's barren fellfield interior.

WILDLIFE

Light-mantled sooty albatrosses are commonly seen soaring along the steep coastal tussac slopes between the gentoo penguin colony at Tortula Cove and Mai Point, where there are also several white-chinned petrel colonies. Elephant seals and fur seals both breed here, the latter aggressively defending their territories in November and December. A few seals even make their way upstream to the lakes which have become popular swimming pools. This is ideal habitat for pintail which nest in the tussac areas around the lakes.

Above Maiviken from the entrance to the sealers' cave
Right The waters of Maivatn cascading down a mossy valley
leading to Maiviken

Facing page Female fur seal with pup

HUMAN HISTORY

The first detailed description of Maiviken was written by Dr J. Gunnar Andersson who remarked upon the beauty of the site while camping here in May 1902, in the company of three other expedition members of Nordenskjöld's Swedish South Polar Expedition (including S. Duse, the cartographer, after whom nearby Mount Duse is named). The party explored Bore Valley, and after passing over the col, descended the southern gradient to discover a superb little harbour. When the Grytviken whaling station was built here two years later, the walk to Maiviken became a regular Sunday outing. A field hut built in 1974, was frequently visited by scientists studying the lakes and vegetation, and today provides a snug retreat for the residents of King Edward Point.

Right Light-mantled sooty albatross on nest

Facing page Walkers heading up Bore Valley from Maiviken, with Larsen Point and the entrance to Cumberland Bay beyond (*left*); Maivatn from 'Dead Man's cairn' in Bore Valley (*right*)

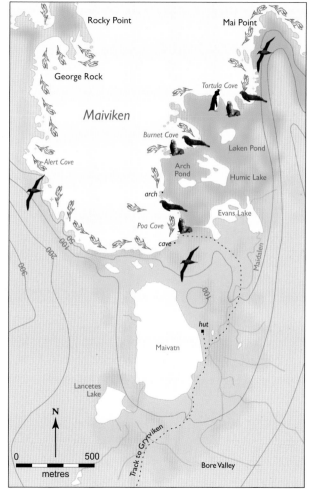

VISITING THE SITE

Whether visiting Maiviken by sea or overland from Grytviken, the bay has the all the makings of a secret hideaway, and to stumble upon the sparkling lakes and small coves tucked away between the cliffs is magical. The best landing site is at the head of Poa Cove near the stream. The sealers' cave is close by, its entrance conspicuously blocked off by a large wooden wall with a door, most likely a 20th century addition to the sparse comfort of a sealers' hearth. Take a flashlight as it is dark inside, and there's a fairly steep step down onto the floor of the cave.

The 3 km track to Grytviken initially follows the stream course inland from the beach in Poa Cove - by far the best way to negotiate a path through fur seal-filled tussac. Once out of the tussac, a steep uphill climb leads to the hut on the east side of Maivatn, and then uphill again over a series of rock outcrops and ridges to the 200 m high saddle at Dead Man's Cairn. From here it is a downhill hike across the Bore Valley scree slopes to Grytviken.

Some areas of fragile mosses and lichens around the lakes are susceptible to trampling, so avoid stepping off the track. Be aware also that during the period of military occupation 1982-2000, Bore Valley was used for live-firing exercises, and despite being checked and cleared, it may still contain debris and possibly unexploded ordnance - another very good reason to keep to the track.

COBBLERS COVE

Includes the plateau to the north of the cove out to Rookery Point, site of a large macaroni penguin colony. Named after the white-chinned petrels (also known as shoemakers or cobblers) which nest here.

FEATURES
▸ Macaroni penguin colony
▸ Sheltered yacht anchorage
  ▸ Zodiac cruise between Cobblers Cove, Rookery Point and Godthul

POINTERS
▸ Zodiac cruising is very weather dependent
▸ Hikers should be aware of giant petrel colony on the plateau

LOCATION AND MAIN FEATURES
Cobblers Cove is situated 8 km east of Cumberland Bay, and about 2 km northwest of Godthul. It is one of the most sheltered yacht anchorages in South Georgia. There is an abundance of wildlife to be found in the area, and notably the macaroni penguin colony at Rookery Point. In the past, it was called Pleasant Cove by British surveyors, Hystadhullet after an early 20th century Norwegian whaling captain by the name of Hystad, and Skomaker Hullet which means cobbler's cove in Norwegian.

The snug anchorage of Cobblers Cove with Godthul in the distance

LANDFORM AND HABITAT

The entrance to Cobblers Cove is a dramatic narrow channel guarded by the 100 m high summit of Long Point. Once inside, the shoreline widens to form a near landlocked kelp-strewn basin bounded on all sides by steep-sided, tussac-clad hillsides, with the exception of the low isthmus that separates the cove from the adjoining bay of Godthul. Reindeer tread well-worn paths leading to their favourite feeding areas near the gentoo penguin colonies, and graze the *Festuca* grassland slopes and coastal tussac areas below the steep scree slopes. On the northern shore of the cove above the shingle landing beach, a scree gully – often filled with snow far into the summer season – leads up to a 150 m high saddle and plateau. From its northern edge, the plateau descends gently to the macaroni penguin colony at Rookery Point.

The coastline from Cobblers Cove to Rookery Point is dominated by 50 m high cliffs of folded jointed sedimentary rocks, excellent examples of the Cumberland Bay Formation. Caves and wave-cut platforms at the base of kelp-fringed cliffs are often battered by ocean swells. Further offshore, the several kelp-covered reefs and conspicuous tussac-covered sea stack of East Skerry are further evidence of the powerful forces that have shaped this coastline.

WILDLIFE

Gentoo penguins occupy colonies on both the northern and southern shores of the cove, and healthy populations of fur seals and elephant seals

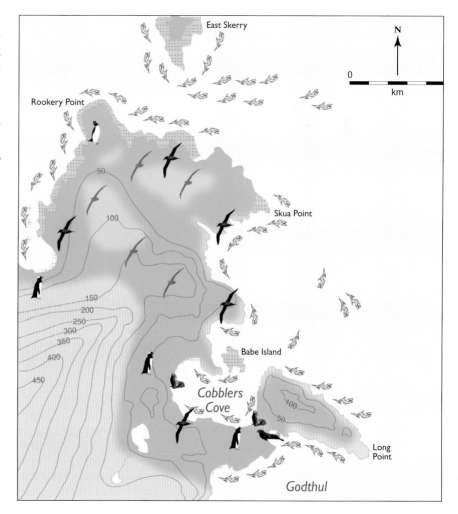

Southern giant petrel (*above*)
and northern giant petrel (*below*)

The most reliable way of differentiating
between these two closely-related species is
by the colour of the bill-tip, being greenish in
southern and reddish in northern.

line the shores, particularly on the isthmus. Light-mantled sooty albatrosses nest along most sections of the coastline and white-chinned petrel burrows can be found on the upper tussac slopes and headlands. These birds have earned the nicknames 'cobblers' and shoemakers because of the noise they make in and around their burrows, similar to that of an old-fashioned cobbler's sewing machine. Dozens of southern giant petrel nests are scattered on the plateau area and there are several thousand pairs of macaroni penguins breeding on the west-facing slopes of Rookery Point overlooking Rookery Bay. From their traditional landing site on the rocky shore, the macaronis waddle purposefully up smooth-surfaced rocks into a network of muddy channels running between the tussac bogs. Standing guard over the colony a pair of skuas can usually be spotted perched on a tussac-fringed rocky outcrop. In addition to penguin eggs and chicks, these birds also hunt blue petrels that nest on the nearby rat-free tussac island of East Skerry and petrel remains such as wings and skulls, are often found in skua middens in this area.

HUMAN HISTORY

There is little recorded human history at this site and no traces of sealers' camps have been found in the cove, although such a safe harbour would have undoubtedly been frequently visited by those early visitors to the island. In nearby Rookery Bay, once known locally as Schomar Bay, a whale catcher of that name foundered there with all hands in 1934.

The cove was charted by John Chaplin and his Royal Navy survey team aboard the motor boat *Alert* during the *Discovery* Investigations in 1929. They camped on the northern shore of the cove for three months, remarking that the cove offered excellent shelter for *Alert*, and it has become a favourite anchorage for many of the yachts visiting the island today.

VISITING THE SITE

Good weather and calm seas are needed for zodiac cruising along the coast between Rookery Bay and Godthul, and even the short section around Long Point when transiting between Godthul and Cobblers Cove can be extremely rough in the backwash of waves bouncing off the cliffs and rock platforms. However, once inside Cobblers Cove, landings are possible in virtually all conditions, the beach on the northern shore being the easiest starting point for a hike to Rookery Point. The initial steep climb from the beach up the scree slope leads to the saddle and thence across the plateau and down towards the macaroni penguin colony, a round distance of about 4 km. The inland slopes are peppered with white-chinned petrel burrows and southern giant petrel nests, so be alert, particularly when traversing the plateau area where many of the giant petrel nests are well hidden amongst the tussac.

Facing page Brown skuas guard their nest on the plateau above Cobblers Cove overlooking Rookery Bay (*above left*); macaroni penguins make the trek from their landing rock to their colony amongst the tussac at Rookery Point (*below left*); orange and yellow crustose lichens can be found on many sheltered rock outcrops, particularly in the vicinity of bird colonies (*right*)

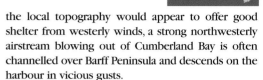

GODTHUL

54°17'S 36° 18'W

The harbour (which means 'good cove' in Norwegian) was probably named by Norwegian sealers and whalers.

FEATURES

▸ The old whaling shore depot
▸ Whale bones on the beach
▸ Hike to the lakes and summit

POINTERS

▸ Reindeer tracks can be steep, muddy and slippery
▸ Do not remove any bones or artefacts
▸ Avoid inadvertently causing reindeer to stampede through the penguin colony
▸ Take care to avoid nesting giant petrels when hiking

LOCATION AND MAIN FEATURES

Situated 9 km east of Cumberland Bay on the eastern shores of Barff Peninsula, Godthul is a 3 km long inlet that lies between Cape George and Long Point. The sugarloaf silhouette of Cape George is a conspicuous landmark, its large rounded summit mirrored in miniature by the headland of Long Point.

Reindeer and gentoo penguins are abundant, and the calls of light-mantled sooty albatrosses echo off the natural cliff amphitheatre that encircles the harbour. A floating factory ship serviced by two whale catchers was stationed here each summer from 1908 to 1917 and again from 1922 to 1929. A small shore depot supporting the whaling operations was established close by a stream in the southeast corner of the harbour, and the rusting barrels, wooden shed and boats are fascinating relics of the whaling era, as is the impressive collection of whale and elephant seal bones scattered along the beach.

LANDFORM, CLIMATE AND HABITAT

The harbour is enclosed within the head walls of a glacial cirque where grass-covered hills rise to extensive scree slopes below a skyline of 500 m high jagged mountain ridges.

Nestling at the foot of the head wall are two lakes fed by numerous meltwater and drainage streams, and at the head of the bay a 30 m high waterfall flows straight over the cliffs into a tidal pool on the rocky foreshore where fur seals often play. Although

the local topography would appear to offer good shelter from westerly winds, a strong northwesterly airstream blowing out of Cumberland Bay is often channelled over Barff Peninsula and descends on the harbour in vicious gusts.

Godthul is interesting geologically, displaying outcrops from both the Cumberland Bay and Sandebugten Formations. The former are apparent along the western shore out to Long Point and again at Cape George itself, while the eastern side comprises Sandebugten Formation rocks. The shoreline is typical of this region of South Georgia, where the coastal foreland slopes gently inland from 20 to 30 m high sea cliffs to terminate against a steep mountain front, and the cliff coastline is fringed with low wave-cut rock platforms, kelp beds, and the occasional cobble and shingle beach.

WILDLIFE

Godthul's gentoo penguin population traditionally occupies the eastern shores of the bay, nesting in groups of upwards of several hundred pairs scattered between the lake above the shore depot and Briggs Point. Large herds of reindeer graze the lush grasses and sheltered hollows that offer the cows and their newborn calves some of the best pasture South Georgia has to offer.

Elephant seals and fur seals are common around the shore depot landing beach, often sleeping in the hut and amid the piles of barrels. Depending on the exact location of colonies in the area, the landing

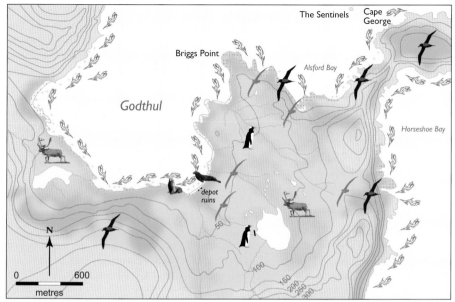

Godthul

Briggs Point

The Sentinels Cape George

Alsford Bay

Horseshoe Bay

depot ruins

N

0   600
metres

50

100

150
200
250
300

Right The gentoo colony at Godthul – each nest a careful pecking distance apart
Far right The spray-drenched waterfall margins provide the perfect damp environment for emerald green mosses to flourish

127

beach may also be crowded with gentoos as they go back and forth to the sea from their nests by the lake. A few pairs of southern giant petrels nest on the slope between the depot and the lake, and towards the saddle overlooking Horseshoe Bay.

HUMAN HISTORY

Whaling operations began at the site on 8th January 1908 when the whaling factory ship *Aviemore* accompanied by two catcher vessels *Edda* and *Snore* anchored in the harbour. These vessels belonged to the Bryde & Dahl Hvalfangerselskab Company in Sandefjord, Norway. The company established a floating factory operation which included a small shore base with a storage shed, three small oil tanks, and a depot of wooden and metal barrels. A dam was built at the nearby lake to provide a reliable supply of fresh water. Wooden boats called *jolles* were used as platforms for flensing whales alongside the factory ship. Still visible today, although partly hidden between the tussac that surrounds the shed and the steel tank, are piles of disintegrating barrels, several wooden boats and an assortment of debris from the whaling era, amid the impressive collection of whale and seal bones strewn along the shore.

VISITING THE SITE

On a calm sunny day, Godthul is a tranquil site with stunning coastal views from the summit ridge overlooking Horseshoe Bay and the head of the bay waterfall, ideal for hikes into the foothills, or for beachcombing in the vicinity of the landing beach - although do resist the temptation to remove whale and seal bones; not only is their removal prohibited but they are an integral historical feature of the site. Take care also to choose your landing site at a distance from the gentoo landing area which is usually near the stream on the south side of the shed.

The quickest and easiest access to the foothills is a direct line from the shed to the lake above, taking care to avoid any nesting giant petrels en route. From the top of the slope, a number of options are available: quiet moments to watch gentoo penguins bathing in the lake; a 1 km walk out to the Briggs Point area and its large groups of gentoos, or a longer climb up the 300 m summit to the northeast and its spectacular views over Horseshoe Bay and Cape George; or follow the reindeer tracks west across the steep tussac slopes at the head of the bay towards the waterfall and tarn. Beware however, as the track passes over some very steep ground.

Some energetic parties have continued from here over a pass that leads to Reindeer Valley and down into Cumberland East Bay, finishing at either Sandebugten or the field hut at nearby Corral Bay, both sheltered pickup points. This hike however is only recommended during periods of settled weather and when accompanied by someone who is familiar with the route.

Left Whale and seal bones surface from beneath the beach shingle after every gale

Facing page On all but the steepest slopes the tussac here has been grazed by reindeer (*above left*); flat bottomed wooden boats or *jolles* – they were moored alongside the whale and used as a platform for flensing floating whale carcassses (*below left*); a large male fur seal settles comfortably amongst the tussac and whaling debris at the shore depot (*right*)

OCEAN HARBOUR

54° 20'S 36° 16'W

Previously called New Fortuna Bay, probably in association with C. A. Larsen's whale catcher Fortuna. *The name changed to Ocean Harbour around 1909 when the ship* Ocean *operated by the Norwegian company Hvalfangerselskab 'Ocean' of Larvik commenced whaling at the site.*

FEATURES
▸ Macaroni penguin colony
▸ Spectacular folded rocks
▸ Kelp forests
▸ Waterfall at head of bay
▸ Wreck of *Bayard*
▸ Locomotive
▸ Oldest recorded grave
▸ Trypot visible at low tide

POINTERS
▸ Wet under foot in the valley behind the whaling station

LOCATION AND MAIN FEATURES

Ocean Harbour lies about 6 km south of Godthul and roughly halfway between St. Andrews Bay and the entrance to Cumberland Bay. Another popular anchorage for yachts, it is one of South Georgia's finest small vessel anchorages, sheltered from all winds, although a heavy easterly swell may set in at times. The whaling station stood at the head of the harbour until 1920 when most of it was removed to Stromness. Only a few visible relics remain, among them a shed, the wreck of *Bayard*, a steam locomotive and a handful of graves. Elephant seals and fur seals abound, and the area is heavily grazed by reindeer.

LANDFORM AND HABITAT

The site is located in one of the sunniest and warmest areas on the island, well protected from westerly winds by the 800 m high massif of the Szielasko Ice Cap. The kelp-fringed harbour is nearly 2 km long, orientated roughly southwest-northeast and ending in a broad sandy beach backed by a large expanse of level ground on a glacial outwash plain that extends nearly 1 km inland. Small braided streams edged with emerald green moss meander across the grassy plain, through the whaling station ruins and into the harbour. Most of the tussac in this bay has been severely over-grazed by reindeer, replaced by moss-covered hummocks interspersed with the introduced annual meadow-grass. The *Festuca*-covered slopes end on a 300 m high ridge

that separates the harbour from Penguin Bay to the south, providing a stark contrast to the austere cliffs of beautifully folded Sandebugten Formation rocks on the opposite shore.

WILDLIFE

One of the highlights here is the sight of over 80 pairs of blue-eyed shags – an exceptionally large colony for South Georgia – comfortably ensconced amid the flourishing stand of tussac that has colonised the decks of *Bayard*. This magnificent riveted iron-hulled three-masted barque complete with bowsprit was built in Liverpool in 1864. Blown from her moorings at the coaling pier on the north side of the bay in 1911, she ran aground on the opposite shore where, despite the attempts of two whale catchers to pull her off, she remained fast.

Herds of reindeer often pass through the valley and across the southern slopes of the harbour;

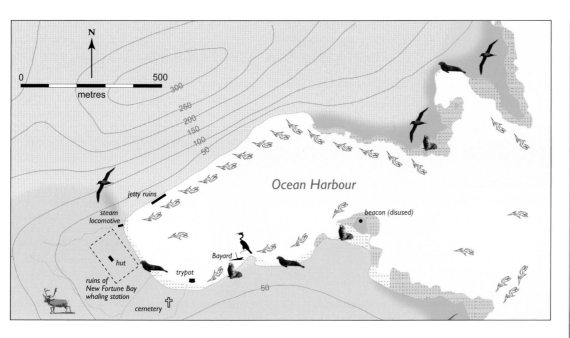

Ocean Harbour

N

0 ——— 500
metres

300
250
200
150
100
50

jetty ruins

steam
locomotive

hut

ruins of
New Fortune Bay
whaling station

cemetery

trypot

Bayard

50

beacon (disused)

Right Previously used for running ropes, these blocks were aptly known as 'Dead Man Eyes' or 'Dead Eyes'
Far right Perched atop the bowsprit of *Bayard*, kelp gulls and shags keep a wary lookout

Facing page Aerial view of Ocean Harbour

kelp gulls roost and nest in the vicinity of the coaling jetty ruins; light-mantled sooty albatrosses nest on sheltered ledges, and pintails flit to and fro between the elephant seal wallows and tidal pools. A traditional haulout beach for elephant seals, fur seals also started breeding here in the late 1990s.

HUMAN HISTORY

South Georgia's earliest recorded grave, that of Frank Cabrail, a steward who died on 14th October 1820 onboard *Francis Allen,* is found here although the exact site of the grave is unknown. Five crosses and at least two unmarked graves can be seen on the southern slopes at the head the bay, and in 1910, a man's skeleton was unearthed; the skull had a bullet hole through it, '*probably a relic of some quarrel*'. Other remnants of the sealers remain including an algae-covered trypot, visible only at low tide.

The licence issued with the lease was the first to stipulate that every part of the whale was to be processed thus making it impossible to operate efficiently with a floating factory, and imposing the construction of a shore station. Fortunately the site was ideal for this task, with its plentiful fresh water supply, sheltered harbour and large expanses of level ground for shore-based installations. Although several stations had winch-, manual- or gravity-powered narrow gauge railways, Ocean Harbour was the only one with a steam locomotive, used to haul cargo between the coaling jetty and the station.

Building at the site began in October 1909 when the ship *Ocean* accompanied by two whale catchers *Penguin* and *Pelican* arrived from Norway. C. A. Larsen's brother, Lauritz, was the first station manager. He apparently kept a riding horse here, and introduced the first reindeer to South Georgia for both sport and fresh meat, landing three stags and seven hinds at the station in 1911. This era also saw the introduction of a postal service for the two Barff Peninsula whaling stations. The mail was delivered by a courier who sailed or rowed the 12 km stretch of water across Cumberland East Bay from Grytviken to the refuge hut at the foot of the Sorling Valley, then hiked overland to Godthul and Ocean Harbour.

Although the Ocean Harbour station was remarkably successful, producing a high return of barrels per whale and thousands of sacks of guano, it closed in 1920 after the merger of Ocean and Sandefjord Havalfangerskab and the formation of a new company, Vestfold Havalfangers A.S. Buildings and equipment were moved to Stromness Harbour, and the remaining ruins and relics are bare outlines among the grass and seals.

VISITING THE SITE

Ocean Harbour's safe anchorage and sandy beaches offer easy landings and pleasant forays amongst the whaling station remnants in the north corner of the bay. If heading inland via the valley behind the station, take care to avoid the wet boggy areas along the stream margins. Keep a sharp look out for some very deep, muddy and smelly wallows and the odd stray fur seal between the tussac bogs at the back of the beach, especially when heading towards the gravesites in the far corner or around to the wreck of *Bayard*.

Left On misty days, as *Bayard* emerges from the mist, she looks eerily underway, heeled over in the wind
Top One of the wooden crosses overlooking site of the New Fortune whaling station
Bottom Early morning mist lifts slowly from the still waters of the harbour

Facing page Tussac flourishes on the rotten wooden decks of *Bayard*, where blue-eyed shags return to nest each year

ST. ANDREWS BAY

54° 26'S 36° 11'W

One of the few places at South Georgia whose place-name origin is unknown.

FEATURES

▸ South Georgia's largest king penguin colony
▸ South Georgia's largest elephant seal beach
▸ Reindeer

POINTERS

▸ Landings are very weather dependent
▸ Rivers are fast flowing and deep
▸ Be aware of breeding terns and skuas on the outwash plains
▸ Do not walk into the king penguin colony
▸ Do not disturb reindeer in the vicinity of the king penguin colony

LOCATION AND MAIN FEATURES

St. Andrews Bay lies approximately 30 km southeast of the entrance to Cumberland Bay. The bay is fully exposed to the open sea and to the strong winds that plummet from the ice-clad summits of the southern end of the Allardyce Range, where the 2,000 m summits of Mt. Roots, Mt. Kling, Nordenskjold Peak and Mt. Brooker form a superb backdrop to the largest concentration of king penguins and elephant seals on the island. The king penguin colony borders the banks of the river that flows from the Buxton and Cook Glaciers about 1 km south of a field hut nestled under the hills at the northern end of the beach. Reindeer often graze in the vicinity of the colony.

LANDFORMS AND HABITAT

The surf-beaten coastline at St. Andrews Bay runs north–south in a 3 km long uninterrupted sweep of fine dark sand, covered in penguins and seals and bounded in the interior by the Cook, Buxton and Heaney Glaciers. The northern entrance point to the bay, Clark Point, extends seaward as a shallow kelp-covered reef, and there are two isolated kelp-encircled shoal patches lying in the northern approaches to the bay.

Thirty years ago, the Cook Glacier terminated at the high water mark on the beach in a spectacular 30 m high, 500 m long ice cliff. Since then, the snouts of all three glaciers have significantly ablated and retreated. The Heaney Glacier is now well over 1 km from the shore line, while the snout of the Cook Glacier is approximately 200 m from the sea and separated from it by a lagoon whose seaward margin is the original St. Andrews Bay coastline. The beach is now reduced to a narrow sand and shingle bar which forms a low protective barrier with a single narrow opening to the sea. The two major melt water rivers issuing from the Buxton and Heaney Glaciers are deep and fast running – and not easy to cross.

The river beds change course seasonally as the flow of water fluxes and wanes, and wave action on the beach affects the position of the river mouths. The formation of an ice-free passage along the beach connecting the Barff Peninsula to the Royal Bay area to the south was of great benefit to the reindeer whose grazing range was increased by at least 25%, with a corresponding increase in population.

The relatively recent period of glacial retreat combined with constant grazing by reindeer has resulted in a very sparse covering of short mixed grassland consisting mainly of annual meadow-grass and some Antarctic hairgrass, small herbs and other native grasses. The meadow-grass thrives in the vicinity of the king penguin colony due to year-round input of nutrient-laden guano. Tussac is rare, being heavily grazed by reindeer in all but the most inaccessible cliffs areas at Clark Point.

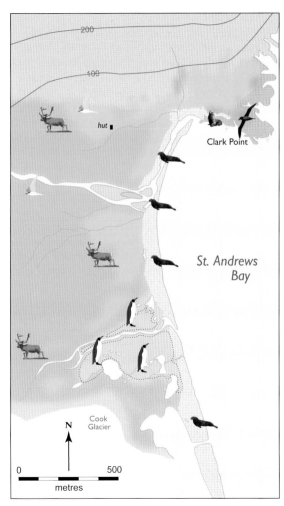

WILDLIFE

The king penguin colony, the largest at South Georgia, was first described in 1883 during a visit by the 1882-83 German International Polar Year expedition. 1,100 birds were recorded there in 1925, when it was believed to be the largest colony on the island. Gerry Clark, a New Zealand ornithologist and sailor (whose name is commemorated by Clark Point) counted 32,000 chicks in the winter of 1985. Seventeen years later, there were approximately 150,000 pairs, a three-fold increase typical of the majority of South Georgia's large king penguin colonies. During October and November the beach is carpeted with elephant seals, with up to 6,000 cows estimated at peak haulout, making St. Andrew's Bay also one of the largest elephant seal breeding beaches on the island.

Such a large assemblage of wildlife attracts an entourage of persistent and voracious scavengers. Sheathbills dart in and around the penguin colony and run the gauntlet amongst the elephant seals; giant petrels lurk on the outskirts, wings outspread and ready to enter the heart of the colony on a raid for healthy chicks; while others bob relentlessly at the beach edge waiting for downy water-logged chicks borne seaward in the fast flowing streams.

Cape petrels nest in small numbers on the cliffs north of St. Andrews Bay and can sometimes be seen rafting in the kelp-strewn waters off Clark Point. Leopard seals patrol the rocks at this end of the beach too, hunting penguins along the edge of the kelp beds. A few white-chinned petrels and light-mantled sooties nest on the tussac slopes at Clark Point. Brown skuas and Antarctic terns breed on the outwash plain and scree slopes at the north end of the beach, defending their nest sites with their characteristic noise and vigour.

HUMAN HISTORY

While the bay was almost certainly sighted by Captain Cook and would subsequently have attracted its share of 19th century blubber-seeking sealers, the first account of explorations in the area date from 1882. More detailed research was carried out by Ludwig Kohl-Larsen's expedition. Camping here in April 1929, they collected specimens and filmed the penguins between bouts of horrendous weather. Their little expedition was one of the first to observe the complex pattern of the king penguin breeding cycle. Over 50 years later in 1981-82 film-makers Cindy Buxton and Annie Price spent five months here filming penguins, working from the comfort of the little field hut, as others have done since, including the BBC Natural History TV Unit filming for the wildlife series 'Life in the Freezer' and 'Blue Planet'.

VISITING THE SITE

Landings at St. Andrews Bay are very much weather dependent. Heavy swell and high winds off the glaciers are not uncommon and rapid and unexpected changes in weather conditions should be anticipated. The far north corner of the beach, tucked in under Clark Point, is the most sheltered landing site.

In terms of wildlife numbers, there are few places that compare with St. Andrews Bay on a sunny spring day when the snow-covered beach is packed with over 6,000 elephant seals and up to 200,000 penguins.

The king colony is an incredible experience – the sheer scale and multitude of the population is overwhelming. As with most penguin colonies, the best way of absorbing the sensory overload is to find a quiet spot and simply sit and observe the birds. By patiently waiting and watching, the true dynamic nature of the colony is revealed, and close-up views of birds are guaranteed as the more curious individuals gather around. This is also the best way to get good views of reindeer as they graze undisturbed by the presence of people. At all costs, avoid disturbing reindeer in the vicinity of the penguins as the animals may stampede directly through the middle of the colony. Also, keep a good distance from the elephant seal harems as some cows are easily frightened.

The view from some of the moraine ridges around the penguin colony is well worth the hike as the true scale of the colony becomes apparent, but take care when crossing the rivers as they may be deep and fast-flowing.

Above left King penguin chicks line the banks of the fast flowing glacial meltwater stream careful not to be jostled in for fear of being washed out to sea
Above right King penguins wash their feathers in the surf before coming ashore to preen and re-coat the feathers with oil

Facing page The small refuge hut is still used by researchers and residents from King Edward Point and Grytviken – be sure to close the door behind you! (*top*);
Antarctic terns breed on the outwash plain and neighbouring slopes (*bottom*)

King penguins

Klemens Pütz,
Antarctic Research
Trust

First encounters with king penguins are unforgettable: the sound and smell of a hundred thousand birds gathered on the beach and by the river at St. Andrews Bay is surpassed only by the spectacle that these beautifully plumaged penguins offer the visitor. Whether in the depths of a snowy winter landscape or beneath the brilliant blue skies of a still summer's day, their characteristic grace, superbly contrasting slate-grey and white feathers, and golden orange 'ear' patches, are captivating.

King penguins breed on sub-Antarctic islands that lie close to or within that body of circumpolar water south of the Polar Front and north of the winter pack-ice edge. South Georgia is their South Atlantic stronghold, with over 400,000 pairs breeding in huge colonies found mainly along the north coast. Their reproductive cycle is unique among penguins since it requires more than one year to raise a chick. Birds that failed to breed successfully the previous year ('early breeders') start courtship in November after they have finished their moult. A single egg is laid in early December and incubated on the bird's feet for 54 days until the chick hatches in late January. Hatchlings are then guarded in turn by one parent while the other forages at sea, returning frequently to provision the chick with food.

Once the chick is six weeks old, it no longer requires the warmth and protection of its brooding parents, thanks to a growing layer of fatty tissue and a fluffy brown coat of downy plumage that contrasts so markedly with the sleek lines of the adults. The chicks gather together in crèches, often along river banks – ribbons of brown amid the mass of grey and orange adults. With both parents now free to forage simultaneously the chick receives double the amount of food and by the end of summer has accumulated the large fat reserves it needs to survive the oncoming winter months. At this time, parents may be away for several weeks as they search the ocean for fish that have become less abundant and are further offshore than in the summer. Meanwhile the chicks huddle together for warmth and shelter, a great body of dark brown on white snow.

With the return of spring, food supplies increase and the chicks are fed more frequently until fledging which starts in December. Successful breeders – those that have raised a chick to fledging – then take a three month break before laying their next egg at the end of summer. Chicks of these so-called 'late breeders' are usually too small at the onset of winter to survive the imminent starvation period and it is only in years of favourable winter feeding that some chicks survive to fledging at the end of the following summer. Thus, although king penguins are able to rear two chicks within three years, they most commonly raise one chick and have one failed breeding attempt over a two year period.

South Georgia kings were studied by Bernard Stonehouse who set up camp with the seal biologist, Nigel Bonner, in 1953 at Ample Bay near Salisbury Plain in the Bay of Isles and unravelled the complexities of their unique breeding cycle. Despite their conspicuous year-round presence ashore, it became apparent that these penguins in fact spend most of their time at sea, where their activities remained a mystery until the recent advent of new technology in the form of miniaturised data loggers. These instruments are attached to the birds' plumage or inserted in their stomachs, storing and transmitting information that tells us where, when and how the penguins feed.

Time depth recorders have told us much about the birds diving behaviour. Their dive profiles reflect the daily migration pattern of myctophid lanternfish, the staple diet of king penguins. These fish swim in dense shoals, moving to the surface at night and returning to the ocean depths in the day, and similarly, the penguins' night dives are no deeper than 30 m, whereas during the day they may reach depths of over 350 m. The duration of such deep dives can exceed seven minutes. Most surprisingly, the surface recovery periods are only about two minutes between dives and the birds are able to make up to seven deep dives in an hour. The physiological adaptations behind these magnificent capabilities are still poorly understood. However during a dive heart beat frequency and blood perfusion is significantly reduced, a physiological adaptation previously known only in seals. Results

from stomach temperature sensors show that more fish are caught during the day at greater depths than during the shallow night dives. These devices also show that towards the end of a foraging trip the temperature of the lower abdomen is maintained well below the average body temperature of 37°C. This is thought to be an adaptation to keep the food as fresh as possible until the meal can be delivered to the chick.

Sophisticated tracking devices have allowed us to follow the birds on their summer foraging trips as they swim the 250 km north to the rich feeding grounds of the Polar Front, travelling distances of up to 100 km a day back and forth to the colony. In winter, the birds are thought to feed at the edge of the pack ice zone, thousands of kilometres and several weeks distant from their breeding site.

How they navigate to and from their remote foraging grounds is still unknown.

As with all penguins, kings go through a 'catastrophic' moult at the end of their breeding season, changing all their feathers in one 14 day period during which they are unable to go to sea and feed (*left*) The chick's initial coat is a thin grey down (*top*) which eventually evolves into a thicker brown coat (*bottom*) which is all that protects it during the cold winter months

MOLTKE HARBOUR

54° 31'S 36° 04'W

The harbour is named after the three-masted steam corvette Moltke *which was the 1882-83 German International Polar Year Expedition vessel and the first powered craft to operate at South Georgia.*

FEATURES

▸ Historic site – ruins of the 1882 German IPY research station
▸ Gentoo penguin colonies

POINTERS

▸ Care should be taken not to disturb any artefacts when visiting the historic site at Köppen Point
▸ Be aware of the presence of nesting southern giant petrels in the vicinity of Köppen Point

LOCATION AND MAIN FEATURES

Moltke Harbour is a scalloped indentation on the northern shore of Royal Bay. Near its eastern entrance at Köppen Point are the ruins of South Georgia's first scientific research station established in 1882 by the German International Polar Year (IPY) Expedition. Whale Valley at the head of the harbour provides easy access to the northern hinterland of Royal Bay.

LANDFORM AND HABITAT

Royal Bay has a reputation of being one of the windiest bays at South Georgia, with squalls of hurricane force recorded off the Ross Glacier. The harbour is also open to the east and subject to swell when the wind is in this quarter, so keep a sharp eye on the weather when visiting this site.

At the head of the harbour is a wide, grey sand beach backed by Whale Valley, which stretches inland for nearly 4 km to the foothills of Mt. Back and Binary Peaks. The extensive valley flats are encased on either side by steep scree slopes, and a network of streams collect in the valley to form 'Whaler-bach' as the Germans called it. Several large roches moutonnées dominate the valley, evidence of a distant era when ice sculpted the land during its retreat inland. Areas of patterned ground with stone stripes and lobes can be seen on the eastern flanks of the valley, and the glaciers are perched between the summit and mountain ridges.

From Whale Valley, the coast runs more or less due east 4 km to Köppen Point and the site of the German IPY station ruins. Remnants of several raised beaches of different heights up to 50 m above sea level can be seen along this coastline, and there are at least three terrace levels in Whale Valley. The shoreline of wave-cut rock platforms is fringed by kelp beds with the occasional small cobble beach backed by low cliffs and sparsely vegetated scree slopes that rise to the 470 m summit of Mt. Krokisius that dominates the northern shore of Royal Bay.

Rocks in the Moltke Harbour area belong to the Sandebugten Formation and show signs of

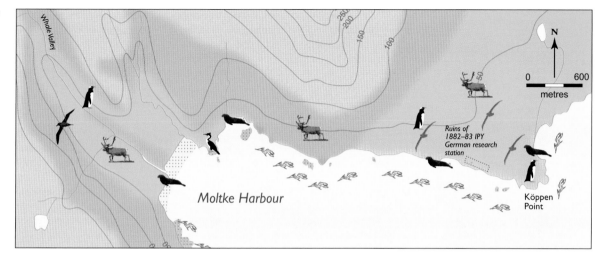

Below left Aerial view of Moltke Harbour looking northwest

Below right Plan of the IPY station based on drawing from Mosthaff, 1890

Facing page The intensity of the small-scale folding of the Sandebugten Formation strata

Whale Valley

Moltke Harbour

Ruins of 1882–83 IPY Gerrman research station

Köppen Point

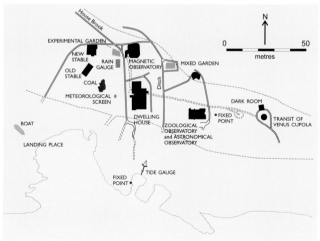

House Brook

EXPERIMENTAL GARDEN

NEW STABLE

RAIN GAUGE

MAGNETIC OBSERVATORY

MIXED GARDEN

OLD STABLE

COAL

Ditch

METEOROLOGICAL SCREEN

BOAT

DWELLING HOUSE

ZOOLOGICAL OBSERVATORY and ASTRONOMICAL OBSERVATORY

FIXED POINT

DARK ROOM

TRANSIT OF VENUS CUPOLA

LANDING PLACE

TIDE GAUGE

FIXED POINT

particularly intense deformation, having undergone substantial metamorphosis. The original thin layers of sandstone and mudstone were first compressed into the large, tight folds seen farther north in Barff Peninsula, and then squashed and buckled into a multiplicity of small folds. As a result the rock outcrops show spectacularly twisted and contorted lines of greywacke and quartz.

The vegetation in the area is singularly unremarkable due to severe over-grazing by reindeer, resulting in most of the tussac, lichens and burnet being replaced by moss and introduced annual meadow-grass. Many former tussac bogs have been reduced to moss-covered mounds, and yellow *Festuca* dominates the rocky scree slopes and drier areas of Whale Valley. Along the stream margins and as far inland as the upper reaches of Whale Valley, a sparse covering of rushes and mosses lends a sombre tone to the landscape.

WILDLIFE

Over 1,000 elephant seal cows haul out on the Moltke Harbour beach at peak pupping in late October. Later in the season, fat sleek weaners congregate by the dozen in sleepy groups at north end of the beach, and swim in the safety of the shallows of the river mouth. Whale Valley, and the coastline leading to the nearby Ross Glacier are the most southerly grazing areas for the Barff Peninsula reindeer herd which expanded from its original grazing grounds north of St. Andrews Bay with the retreat of the Cook Glacier in the early 1960s. A few light-mantled sooty albatrosses nest on the higher outcrops of the western slopes and gentoo penguins criss-cross the valley en route to their colony about 1 km inland, still in more or less the same location recorded by the German IPY expedition (see map, page 35). Sadly, the pipits and most of the burrowing petrels that nested here in 1882 are gone, displaced by a thriving population of rats.

Köppen Point itself is a 50 m high headland with areas of lightly grazed tussac. White-chinned petrel burrows are found here and on some of the headlands to the west. Gentoo penguins and numbers of southern giant petrels nest on the point and on the slopes to the northwest of the station ruins. Very few fur seals currently occupy the site, with no pups recorded so far.

HUMAN HISTORY

Moltke Harbour is one of the few historic sites at South Georgia, outside the whaling stations, where human history truly comes alive. Well before the advent of whaling, the German IPY Expedition established a magnetic observatory here and spent a year studying the region. The scientific programme was determined mainly by the requirements of the International Polar Year which focussed on astronomical, meteorological, geomagnetic, gravimetric and tidal observations and required that data be recorded on the longitude diametrically opposite to an established magnetic observatory in Australia. South Georgia was selected as the site, but the exact location of the station was ultimately determined by the weather. The expedition vessel *Moltke* arrived in Cumberland Bay on 17th August but was blown out by high winds which prevented any landing until 20th August when the vessel was able to enter Royal Bay. Just why the Köppen Point site with its kelp- and rock-strewn approaches was chosen in preference to the easier landing at Whale Valley is unknown, but it is likely that any disadvantages were far outweighed by sheer manpower in the form of 100 seamen who discharged all cargo, cleared over a metre of snow from the site (it was the middle of winter) and built the station in less than two weeks. On completion, the settlement consisted of living quarters for 11 men and their pet dog 'Banquo', magnetic and astronomical observatories with a revolving cupola to observe the transit of Venus, a dark room, laboratory, stables for 17 sheep, nine goats and three oxen – some of which had the full run of the extensive tussac grasslands below Mt. Krokisius in the summer months – and a vegetable garden where potatoes, cereal crops and salad vegetables were grown. With scientists carrying out comprehensive geological, glaciological, hydrographic, biological and topographical surveys of the area as well as the daily weather and geomagnetic observations, this expedition's contribution to our knowledge of South Georgia was outstanding. After their departure in September 1883, the station was abandoned, with the exception of a short stay by the Filchner Expedition in 1911, and occasional visits from passing sealers and whalers.

VISITING THE SITE

With the plan of the station to guide you around the site (page 141), you may imagine the snow-covered landscape that greeted the men on their arrival, followed by the gradual greening of the country as spring advanced. There were gardens to be tended once the ground thawed and snow had melted, goats to be milked, animals to be fed, watered and occasionally butchered. Many of the artefacts from the site are on display in the South Georgia Museum, but you can still see the remains of the coal pile, the drainage ditches, the rusting steel framework of the cupola and the large granite blocks on which instruments were mounted. The site is often occupied by elephant seals dozing between the remnant tussac bogs and in the muddy pools, and their movements, like those of fur seals, occasionally expose historic artefacts in the peaty soil.

Small boat landings below the station ruins can be tricky and should only be attempted in calm conditions, as the shallow wave-cut rock platform provides plenty of lethal obstacles for propellers. The beach at Moltke Harbour is a considerably easier landing site for small boats, providing there is no swell. However, the walk from here to Köppen Point is nearly 4 km across the scree and rock slopes under Mt. Krokisius, and while the reindeer tracks are usually reliable indicators of stable terrain, hikers need to take care when following paths that pass close to cliff edges. For the less energetic, there's an easy, gentle stroll up Whale Valley following the river past the gentoo penguin colony. And if you're there in December on a sunny day, take the time sit and watch the weaners playing in the water at the river mouth.

WILL POINT & BRISBANE POINT

54° 32'S 36°00'W

*This site covers the coastline between Will Point and Brisbane Point.
Will Point was named after Dr. Hermann Will, botanist of the German IPY Expedition 1882-83.
Brisbane Point was named after Matthew Brisbane, second in command on James Weddell's 1823 expedition.*

FEATURES
▸ Large king penguin colony
  ▸ Breeding elephant seals

POINTERS
▸ Very difficult to land
▸ Avoid disturbing the giant petrels at Will Point

LOCATION AND MAIN FEATURES

Will Point is a prominent headland lying on the southern shores of Royal Bay, about 5 km directly across the water from Köppen Point and 5 km east of the Ross Glacier. Southeast of Will Point, the coastline is indented by a 2 km long fjord, Beaufoy Cove, which was formed by the recent retreat of the Weddell Glacier. Brisbane Point is the western entrance point to the fjord, and site of a large king penguin colony. Elephant seals breed along the 1 km stretch of shingle beach between the two points, and light-mantled sooty albatrosses, southern giant petrels, gentoo penguins and pintails nest on the tussac slopes above. The coastline offers no protection from the gale-force winds that often descend the Ross Glacier, and landings are near impossible in all but calm conditions. Nonetheless a zodiac cruise along the beach is very rewarding and for those lucky enough to get ashore, the view from the top of the moraine ridge overlooking the king penguin colony at Brisbane Point is superb.

LANDFORM, CLIMATE AND HABITAT

The Royal Bay scenery is dominated by the Ross Glacier and its 30 m high snout which floats in deep water at the head of the bay. The glacier leads to the Ross Pass, a narrow gap in the island's mountain chain and meeting point of the Allardyce and Salvesen Ranges. At over 600 m altitude, the pass also connects the Ross Glacier to the Brögger Glacier which tumbles down into Undine South Harbour on the south coast. The pass is a natural sledging route across the island, but becomes a wind-tunnel of blizzards and white-outs in westerly gales blows and gives Royal Bay its reputation as one of the windiest places on the island.

The coastal slopes backing the beach between Will Point and Brisbane Point are covered in lush, green tussac with patches of *Festuca* grassland and luxuriant burnet, in marked contrast to the reindeer-cropped vegetation on the north shore of Royal Bay. At Brisbane Point, a prominent tussac-covered moraine ridge forms a conspicuous dividing line between the sand and shingle beach and a large glacial outwash plain created the retreat of the Weddell Glacier. Beyond lies Beaufoy Cove which is separated from Royal Bay by a

Snowy sheathbills dart in and out of the colony, ceaselessly feeding on abandoned eggs and chicks, the dead, the dying and the decomposing (*top*); pebbles from the shingle ridge (*bottom*)

Facing page The king penguin colony encircles several fresh water pools

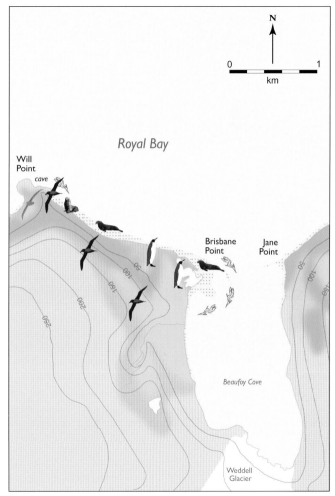

shallow submerged moraine barrier, marked by surf and patches of kelp. It stretches across the mouth of the fjord and links Brisbane Point with a small moraine ridge on the eastern side of the fjord at Jane Point. The moraine was formed during a temporary halt in the retreat of the glacier from its position in 1882 when the snout terminated on the beach at Brisbane Point.

WILDLIFE

The most prominent feature at the site is the huge king penguin colony. This colony, like many others at South Georgia, has undergone a dramatic increase in the past 30 years. It is now estimated at over 30,000 pairs. The colony is concentrated along the beach and at the foot of a steep tussac-covered moraine ridge. On days of heavy surf, the penguins' arrivals and departures are a thrilling spectacle as they negotiate the breakers.

Occasionally, the odd macaroni penguin will turn up amongst the kings, having strayed from colonies along the south shores of Royal Bay. Light-mantled sooty albatrosses nest along the inland tussac slopes and out on the cliffs at Will Point. Elephant seals line the beach towards Will Point, and there are also a few breeding fur seals in the caves and under the cliffs at point itself. On the grassy headlands above are about 50 breeding pairs of southern giant petrels and a few northern giant petrels.

HUMAN HISTORY

Royal Bay was discovered and named by Captain Cook on 18th January during his passage eastwards along the north coast in 1775. Cape George was charted as the bay's western entrance point, and Cape Charlotte as its the eastern point, named after King George III and his consort, Queen Charlotte respectively. Signs of sealers' habitation have been found in the caves at Will Point, and the scattering of elephant seal bones in the area are the last vestiges of the sealing era which ended in the early 1960s.

Royal Bay was first charted in detail by the 1882-83 German IPY Expedition, and it has been visited by many survey expeditions since, including William Filchner's *Deutschland* expedition, Frank Wild on the *Quest*, Kohl-Larsen's expedition in 1929 and Duncan Carse's South Georgia Survey team between 1951-57.

VISITING THE SITE

Zodiac cruising along the shoreline is spectacular, with a rich tapestry of colours provided by the sea, land, tussac and wildlife, and the activity of the king penguins in the surf. Landings on this section of shoreline are usually thwarted by swell, but in calm conditions, it is possible to enter Beaufoy Cove by zodiac, although skill and extreme care are needed to avoid hitting the many submerged rocks that bar the entrance. Remember also, that getting back out again is considerably more difficult if wind and sea conditions increase! Once inside the fjord, the waters are completely calm. From the landing site on the south shore of Brisbane Point, a short walk over level ground brings you to the king penguin colony.

Left The northern shore of Royal Bay from Will Point

Right The sweep of the shingle beach from Will Point running northwest to Brisbane Point

GOLD HARBOUR

54°37'S 35° 56'W

Filchner's German Antarctic Expedition called the bay 'Goldhafen', perhaps because of the iron pyrites or 'fools gold' they found in the local rocks in 1911. Early sealers knew it as Anna's Harbour and it was part of the stretch of coastline that James Cook charted as Sandwich Bay.

FEATURES
▸ King penguin colony
▸ Breeding elephant seals
▸ Light-mantled sooty albatrosses

POINTERS
▸ Walk slowly when on the beach and avoid crowding wildlife
▸ Be aware of king penguin colony boundaries
▸ Be careful of fur seals hidden in tussac
▸ Take care not to approach the tern colony

LOCATION AND MAIN FEATURES

Gold Harbour lies at the foot of the Salvesen Range, about 20 km north of Cape Vahsel. It is regarded by many as one of South Georgia's most beautiful visitor sites. An amphitheatre of hanging glaciers and vertical cliffs rises straight out of the sea and the towering snow-covered peaks of Mt. Paterson create an unforgettable backdrop to an exceptional abundance of seabirds and seals. King penguins, gentoo penguins and elephant seals jostle for space on the beach, and light-mantled sooty albatrosses soar the cliffs out towards Gold Head.

LANDFORM AND HABITAT

Glacialogically, the area is vibrantly active as the Bertrab Glacier continues its rapid retreat. As recently as 1985, its snout terminated on a shingle beach which ran the entire length of the harbour. It has since retreated nearly 1 km inland, and is now separated from the sea by a lagoon and a wave-swept moraine marking the position of the former coastline. Fragments of ice continue to thunder into the sea, creating huge waves and leaving a flotilla of bergy bits and growlers, while meltwater streams cascade gloriously down the cliff face.

The landing beach is in the northern corner of the bay close to the Gold Head cliffs, and while fairly sheltered, there are days when swell breaks the length of the shoreline, and landings are very 'wet'. At this end of the beach, the tectonic contact zone between Sandebugten Formation and Cumberland Bay Formation rocks is visible. On the eastern side of the tectonic contact zone, at Gold Head, the Sandebugten Formation rocks are intensely deformed and contain large pods of dolerite and cubes of iron pyrites or 'fools gold' up to about 5 mm across. The sedimentary layering of the Cumberland Bay Formation rocks on the other side of the contact zone is particularly well-defined on the cliff face that has been recently exposed by the retreat of the Bertrab Glacier.

Behind the beach is a large glacial outwash plain covered in dense coastal tussac that extends inland to the foot of steep slopes of tussac, burnet and scree. The plain is flanked by moraine ridges, and riddled with small streams and pools which coalesce as they head seaward, breaching the beach near the landing site. A second larger stream flows from a lake at the foot of the Bertrab Glacier, through the king penguin colony and meets the sea at the southern end of the beach. The glacier margins and shores of the lagoon are barren expanses of glacial debris with a sparse scattering of lichens, mosses and the introduced annual meadow-grass.

North of the harbour is a vast landscape of undulating hills that extends from Gold Head to Bjornstadt Bay.

WILDLIFE

The king penguin colony, numbering around 25,000 breeding pairs, spills over into the tussac below the conspicuous moraine ridge that dominates the

southern end of the beach. In October–March, the colony is compactly contained along the river margins and upper edge of the beach as incubating birds stand motionless with newly laid eggs. The colony edges are fringed with brown, fluffy chicks and many gather in huge crèches at the edge of the colony close to the landing site. As the season progresses, the parents come and go daily to feed their growing chicks, and non-breeders and pre-breeders come ashore to moult. The beach is then filled to capacity as the kings intermingle with several hundred elephant seals and their pups.

Approximately 300 pairs of gentoo penguin nest here in several groups among the tussac behind the beach, with the usual pair of brown skuas nearby. On the grasslands above the landing beach is a large Antarctic tern colony and southern giant petrels nest on the hilltops above Gold Head. The cliffs are a favourite breeding site for light-mantled sooty albatrosses and their eerie two-toned call can frequently be heard against the background

hum of the king penguin colony. A hike up the steep slope behind the beach and out towards Gold Head, or a zodiac cruise along the foot of the cliffs is often rewarded with spectacular views of these elegant birds as they inspect traditional cliff ledge nest sites, renew pair bonds and engage in their exquisite synchronised courtship flight.

By December most of the elephant seal pups have been weaned and are left to loll about on the sand for three to four weeks before heading out to sea. They can be very inquisitive and will investigate anything or anyone sitting on the beach. The sheer number of seals on the beach during this 'weaner' period is impressive.

Fur seals are most likely to be found in the vicinity of the landing site, playing in the surf and lounging around in the tussac. Few breed here but non-breeding males start hauling out in large numbers towards the end of January, and care should be taken when climbing up the slope towards Gold Head. They often sleep amongst the overhanging tussac, and the only warning of their presence, if you are lucky, may be a low snoring.

HUMAN HISTORY

The first scientific survey of the area was made in 1911 by scientists from Wilhelm Filchner's German expedition. Another visit was made in 1912 by David Ferguson, a geologist contracted by Christian Salvesen & Co. Ltd. to prospect for economic minerals around the island. In 1958, the first hydrographic survey of the harbour was completed on board the RRS *John Biscoe*, and the marine chart produced is still in

use today. During the 1970s, Russian fishing vessels were often seen sheltering in the harbour, but today by far the greatest number of visitors to the bay are cruise ships, with over 2,000 people landing here each year.

VISITING THE SITE

A dawn landing in Gold Harbour is simply overwhelming: the early morning light and sheer numbers and density of wildlife on the beach is incomparable and well worth a 4 am start. Virtually all the wildlife can be seen from within a few metres of the landing site. Walking slowly and being constantly aware of where you are in relation to the wildlife is essential. Early in the season, it is possible to pass along the seafront below the king penguin colony to reach the south end of the beach, and then climb the tussac-covered moraine ridge with its fabulous views of the king penguin colony on one side, and the inner bay and lake on the other.

Later in the season however, when king penguins and elephant seals are spread along the entire length and breadth of the beach, it is preferable to walk through the tussac directly above the landing site (keeping an eye open for pintails feeding in the pools, and the occasional fur seal lurking behind a bog) to the steep slopes at the back of the tussac plain. From here, walk along the foot of the slopes to the lake below the glacier and then out to the moraine ridge. During January and February there are increasing numbers of moulting kings occupying the streams so take care to avoid these and give the gentoo penguins plenty of space.

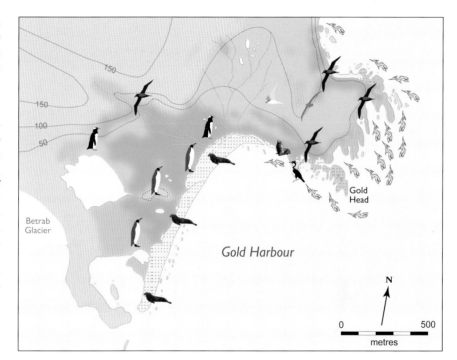

A hike on the hills at the north end of the bay may bring you close to the large tern colony, so listen out for their warning calls and be prepared to back off. Be alert too for giant petrels nesting in this area. The view north to the hilltops above Gold Head is stunning, a panorama of coastline running from Bjornstadt Bay and beyond, and with luck, you may catch a glimpse of light-mantled sooty albatrosses soaring past.

COOPER BAY

54 47'S 35 48'W

*Named after Robert Cooper,
First Lieutenant on board
James Cook's HMS Resolution
during the voyage of
exploration that charted the
coastline and waters in the
vicinity of Cooper Island in
January 1775.*

FEATURES

▶ Chinstrap penguin colony
▶ Macaroni penguin colony
   ▶ Light-mantled sooty
     albatrosses

POINTERS

▶ Avoid crowding wildlife
▶ Be aware of the edge of
   penguin colonies
   ▶ Be careful of fur seals
     hidden in tussac
▶ Minimise vessel lights at
   night to avoid the risk of
     bird strike

LOCATION AND MAIN FEATURES

Cooper Bay at the southeast extremity of the island lies on the south-facing coast of a 5,000 hectare peninsula contained between the Twitcher Glacier in Iris Bay and the Salomon Glacier in Hamilton Bay. It is protected from the open ocean by nearby Cooper Island and enjoys a comparatively mild climate in the lee of the ice-clad summits of the Salvesen Range.

Within the bay are three main beaches. 'Albatross Cove' is the most sheltered, with an all-weather landing beach and safe anchorage for shallow draft yachts.

There is a wealth of wildlife at this site, in a spectacular setting. The island's largest chinstrap colony is found here; gentoo and macaroni penguins dot the tussac slopes and there are plenty of fur seals on the beaches. King penguins, pintails, giant petrels and light-mantled sooty albatrosses are regular breeders, and despite the presence of rats, pipits from nearby rat-free Cooper Island are frequent visitors. There is a large burrowing petrel population on Cooper Island and ships are encouraged to leave the area before nightfall to avoid bird strikes (see page 12).

LANDFORM AND HABITAT

In comparison with the Antarctic-like scenery of nearby Cape Disappointment, Cooper Bay is an oasis of greenery. Situated in the lee of the Salvesen Range, it often enjoys days of tranquil sunshine while gale-force winds are sweeping Drygalski Fjord to the west and Iris Bay to the north.

Cooper Bay straddles the most important geological break in South Georgia – the Cooper Bay Dislocation Zone. To its northeast are sedimentary rocks similar to those of the Sandebugten Formation at Gold Harbour, tightly folded and containing large dolerite pods. In contrast, the southwest side of the bay is mostly igneous rock of the Drygalski Fjord Complex. Cooper Bay itself lies between the two formations in a zone where a sideways, horizontal movement of at least several kilometres created very tight folds marked by stretching and shearing.

The shores of the bay are fringed with kelp beds and bordered by a series of grey gravel and sand beaches, backed by low tussac hillocks and a network of streams. Above this, steep tussac slopes and rock outcrops form a vast amphitheatre of sheer rock and a stunning backdrop to the three coves nestled below. The tussac habitat is a patchwork of varying shades of green, ranging from lush dark green in the vicinity of nutrient-rich seabird and seal concentrations, to hues of yellow on the upper slopes. At about 100 m altitude, the tussac gives way to fellfield – a mosaic of scattered mosses, lichens and occasional small herbs on scree slopes and rocky bluffs.

The landscape of the Cooper Bay area has been sculpted from rock and ice over the last 5,500 years of glacial retreat. The large outwash plain in

Chinstrap porpoising

'Centre Cove' may have formed in the early stages of this retreat, and the Quensel Glacier is the final remnant of ice from this era. Its gently sloping snout terminates over 1 km from the sea and is covered in grey morainic debris. On sunny days the glacial outflow river which flows seaward to the northern corner of 'Main Bay' from beneath the glacier and past a maze of abandoned meltwater channels and moraine ridges, becomes a grey raging torrent laden with fine glacial flour that turns the waters of the bay milky.

WILDLIFE

Four species of penguin breed at Cooper Bay. Macaroni and chinstrap penguins are the most abundant. Over 10,000 pairs of the latter breed in a single colony near the southern entrance point. In November 2004, an outbreak of avian cholera was reported at the colony and the beach closed to visitors. There are many thousands of macaroni penguins on the steep slopes of a small bay to the

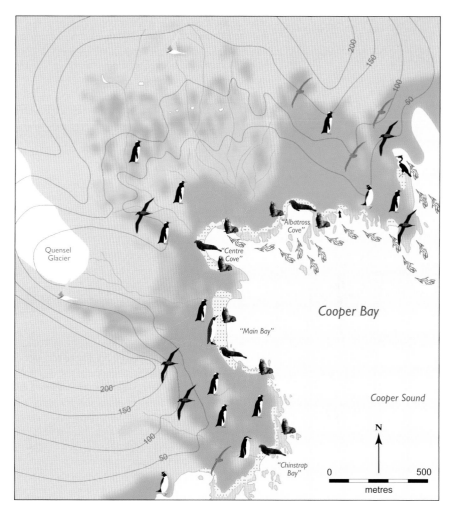

Quensel Glacier

"Albatross Cove"

"Centre Cove"

Cooper Bay

"Main Bay"

Cooper Sound

"Chinstrap Bay"

N

0   500

metres

Top The skua's powerful hooked bill is ideal for ripping and tearing carrion
Bottom During the breeding season the blue-eyed shag sports an electric blue ring around its olive brown eye and yellow caruncles or knobs at the top of its bill. Both fade as the breeding season progresses

west of the chinstraps and a second smaller colony within Cooper Bay itself, 200 m east of 'Albatross Cove', the only macaroni penguin colony at South Georgia that is reasonably accessible from an all-weather landing beach.

The total gentoo penguin population of the Cooper Bay area in 2002 was around 4,000 pairs, making it one of the island's largest breeding areas for this species. At the back of the beach in 'Main Bay' is a small colony of about 250 pairs of king penguins hidden in the tussac, and groups of moulting kings can often be seen along the foreshore. With so many penguins around, the brown skua and sheathbill populations are well provisioned, and pairs occupy traditional nest sites in the vicinity of each colony.

The tussac slopes behind 'Main Bay' and around the chinstrap colony area are favourite nesting areas for South Georgia pintail. These ducks may also be seen feeding along the stream margins at the back of 'Centre Cove' and in the pools at the foot of the Quensel Glacier.

On the glacial debris slopes on the south side of the glacier's snout is a large colony of Antarctic terns. A second colony is found on the highest inland tussac knoll at the back of 'Centre Cove'. In total they contain several hundred breeding pairs, making this one of the island's most important breeding sites for terns.

Light-mantled sooty albatrosses and white-chinned petrels nest in their dozens around the bay, favouring the tussac-covered inland slopes above 'Main Bay' and 'Centre Cove' and the cliff ledges east of 'Albatross Cove'. Southern giant petrels nest in scattered groups above the cove. South Georgia pipits frequently fly over from nearby rat-free Cooper Island, and a few pairs have even been recorded nesting.

Blue-eyed shags are often seen feeding in Cooper Sound and are frequent visitors to the inshore waters of Cooper Bay and there are several colonies in the vicinity of Cape Vahsel and the south coast of Cooper Island.

Elephant Seals breed and moult on all three sand and shingle beaches in the bay. Fur seals are common along most of the coastline, although the highest density of breeding animals is on the beaches and rocky foreshores of 'Centre Bay' and 'Albatross Cove'

HUMAN HISTORY

Glimpses of Cooper Bay in the early 1800s come from one of the few books to be written by a seaman and sealer – *A Narrative of the Life, Travels and Sufferings of Thomas W. Smith.* Smith was an Englishman who signed on as an apprentice on several sealing vessels. In 1818, he was on board *Norfolk* of London in company with the schooner *Ann,* bound for South Georgia and an elephant sealing voyage. This was Smith's second visit to '*that desolate island, unfit for human beings to inhabit*'. He reported that Cooper Bay was '*the only suitable place for a shallop to come to anchor*' at the eastern end of the island, and describes how a sloop and *Ann* '*on her voyage round the island, came into this harbour in consequence of adverse winds'*. That night three men were lost when a '*heavy swell and a strong breeze setting into the harbour'*, caused the sloop to drift on shore where it was totally wrecked. '*After collecting the useful remains of the wreck, and all the blubber that it was possible for us to save'* Smith and the other survivors embarked on the schooner *Ann* to rejoin *Norfolk* for a short voyage to the South Sandwich Islands.

VISITING THE SITES

Although all-weather landings are possible in 'Albatross Cove', access to this landing beach and adjacent tussac areas between November and February can be difficult due to the high density of fur seals. On landing and when hiking in the interior, keep an eye open for seals in the tussac and take care not to block the access routes of penguins to and from the sea. Similarly, when zodiac cruising in the vicinity of the nearby macaroni colony, manoeuvre slowly when close inshore and avoid landing on the small beach directly below the colony. Landings are possible on a small beach between 'Albatross Cove' and the macaroni colony landing beach (see map, page 153), although visitor space is limited, especially during the fur seal breeding season or if the beach and adjacent scree slope are occupied by gentoos, as happens some years.

The route up to the macaroni colony is steep and passes through dense tussac. Small guided groups and rubber boots are essential, and great care is needed in order to avoid disturbing fur seals and penguins. Hikers should be aware of nesting giant petrels, gentoos and skuas in the tussac areas above the macaroni colony.

Zodiac cruising to see the macaronis is encouraged, since the colony is surrounded by deep mud and the penguins are mostly obscured by dense tussac.

Like gentoos and chinstraps, the macaroni penguin uses its pink feet and underside of flippers to radiate excess heat on warm sunny days

Fur Seals

Callan Duck,
Sea Mammal
Research Unit

South Georgia's fur seals (*Arctocephalus gazella* or Antarctic fur seal) are now reckoned to be one of the most numerous seals in the world. Although the exact size of the South Georgia population in 2004 is not known, some scientists estimate that it may exceed three million animals. This is a spectacular recovery from near-extinction in the 19th century when the seals were hunted remorselessly for their valuable pelts. At the time of Cook's visit in 1775, South Georgia was probably the global population centre for the species, but by the late 1800s only a few isolated pockets of animals remained, no doubt on some of the more remote coasts and off-lying islands such as the Willis Islands and Clerke Rocks – areas which were as difficult to access for the early sealers as they are today. One possible contributing factor to the fur seals' spectacular recovery may be the increased availability of krill that followed the 20th century decline of the main krill consumers, the large baleen whales.

Fur seals belong to the otariid or 'eared' seal group. Along with sea lions, they have small but conspicuous rolled ears. In the water, they use their large fore flippers for propulsion, and their hind flippers for steering. On land they walk or run on their fore and hind flippers – and can move faster than most people can run.

South Georgia's fur seals begin their breeding season in early November when the males (bulls) return to traditional breeding beaches and establish small breeding territories. The most favoured areas are just above the upper limit of high tide on both rocky foreshores and shingle beaches.

By mid-November, the best positions on the beach are fully occupied and vigorously defended by these 200 kg males in prime condition. Competition between bulls for territories and females is intense and the resulting fights often lead to serious injuries. Certain beaches and stream beds may be littered with fur seal bones, mostly those of adult males that have succumbed to infections from bite wounds.

The first females (or cows) come ashore in mid-November, and are immediately appropriated by the resident bull, who may have up to 15 females in his harem. Many females return to the same beach area year after year, and give birth to a single pup within two days of hauling out. Approximately one in every 800 pups has a white coat and very occasionally twins may be born. The mother suckles her pup for the next five to eight days before coming into oestrus, when she is mated, usually with the bull in whose territory she resides. Following mating, she departs to sea on the first of her foraging trips which may last between five and eight days depending on the availability and accessibility of krill swarms. She then returns ashore for one to two days to feed her pup, and the alternation of foraging and suckling bouts continues until the pup is weaned at about four months of age.

The ability of a female to find her pup on a crowded beach is remarkable. She begins calling while swimming towards the shore and numerous pups respond. Although recognition is based on the vocalisations between mother and pup established immediately after birth, it is also facilitated by the fact that both animals home in on that area of the beach where they were last together. Eventually the mother isolates her pup and confirms the identification using scent cues. Once the pup is more agile, the mother may move to a less crowded location, often establishing a favourite site for feeding her pup in the tussac grass at the back of the breeding beach.

Pups are weaned in late March or early April, and satellite tracking studies show that the females then head north towards the rich feeding grounds of the Polar Front and remain at sea during the winter months. They are capable of diving to over 150m depth but since their food is almost exclusively on krill, most feeding dives are to 50m only. Males are known to haul out around the island throughout the year, although some head south to feed at the edge of the winter pack ice.

The expansion of the Antarctic fur seal population is having significant repercussions on other wildlife and vegetation and also on human visitors to South Georgia. The coastal tussac grassland and immediate hinterland is being increasingly subjected to trampling damage caused by the repeated passage of seals, and in places, tussac plants have eroded away completely, leaving mud and bare rock. Any burrowing petrels that may have been nesting in the vicinity are long gone. At some wandering albatross breeding locations, seal disturbance has resulted in a redistribution of nest sites. Only the older well-established pairs continue to nest in areas of intense fur seal activity. Likewise, fur seals also present problems for people, and many visitors now prefer the relative peace and safety of an inflatable dinghy cruising close inshore rather than disturbing animals and running the risk of being bitten during a landing at the peak of fur seal breeding.

Scientists so far have been unable to predict future population trends for South Georgia's fur seals. However, there appears to be no sign that the population expansion is waning. And with no apparent shortage of food availability, nor of potential breeding space, there is every likelihood that the Antarctic fur seal population has not yet attained its peak, both in terms of numbers and of the changes it is causing to South Georgia's coastal environment.

Above The relatively few blonde fur seals stand out dramatically against their dark-coated neighbours

Facing page Fur seals spend hours snoozing and snoring away in the tussac, curled up on a tussac bog above the muddy ground

The sheen on this male's coat (*facing page, top*) and on this female's (*top*) demonstrates how hydrodynamic their fur becomes when wet
Fur seal pups, even when only a few days old are already extremely territorial (*right*)

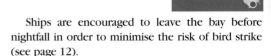

DRYGALSKI FJORD AND LARSEN HARBOUR

58° 50'S 36° 00'W

Drygalski Fjord was named after Professor Erich von Drygalski, leader of the German Antarctic Expedition 1901–03.
Larsen Harbour celebrates the memory of Carl Anton Larsen, pioneer of the South Georgia whaling industry.

FEATURES
▸ Spectacular scenery
▸ Unusual geology
▸ Weddell seals
▸ Snow petrels

POINTERS
▸ Rat-free area
▸ Avoid disturbing the Weddell seals
▸ Take care when walking on scree in the vicinity of seabird burrows
▸ Minimise vessel lights at night to prevent bird strikes

LOCATION AND MAIN FEATURES

Drygalski Fjord lies about halfway between Cooper Bay and Green Island off Cape Disappointment at the southeast extremity of the island. Larsen Harbour is entered on the south side of the fjord and is a narrow steep-sided inlet, 4 km long. Ice and rock dominate the alpine alandscape. Spectacular peaks rise directly out of the sea to over 1,000 m altitude, and magnificent glaciers are still at work carving deep valleys, sharp-pointed glacial horns and arêtes. There is a bewildering mix of rocks of igneous and volcanic origin in this region, some of which are the oldest on the island. There are no rats here, so pipits and burrowing petrels are present wherever there is suitable tussac habitat, and the area is a stronghold for snow petrels.

Ships are encouraged to leave the bay before nightfall in order to minimise the risk of bird strike (see page 12).

LANDFORM and HABITAT

Drygalski Fjord is 14 km long, and follows the northwest-southeast orientation of the peaks of the Salvesen Range (Mt. Carse, Mt. Macklin, Douglas Crag and Trendall Crag) which rise to over 2,000 m barely 5 km from the sea. These mountains and the northern shore of the fjord are composed of the Drygalski Fjord Complex rocks. Once part of the continental margin of Gondwana, they are the oldest rocks on South Georgia, and consist of schists and gneisses with intrusions of a variety of granites and gabbros, cut by dolerite intrusions.

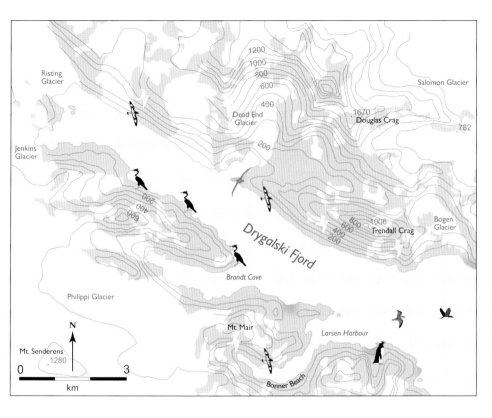

Left Looking down into Larsen Harbour and Bonner Beach from the pass over to Esbensen Bay

Facing page Precipitous ice-covered mountains and glaciers are typical of this area (*left*);
Dolerite dykes cutting across banded gabbro on the northeast coast of Drygalski Fjord (*right*)

Below Bearded lichens (*Usnea* sp.) are characteristic of high altitude fellfield
Bottom Weddell seals breed at Bonner Beach and Laws Beach in Larsen Harbour

Facing page Snow petrels (*left*) and Antarctic terns (*right*) are abundant in Drygalski Fjord, feeding in the upwellings at the glacier fronts and the snow petrels wheeling off their cliff ledge nest sites high up the fjord (*left*); Glacial streams (*below*) cascade to the sea all along the fjord, an easily accessible source of fresh water for visiting yachts

A fault zone running the length of the fjord separates these rocks from those of the Larsen Harbour Complex on the fjord's southern shore. Relics of an ancient ocean floor formed by volcanic activity in an expanding submarine basin, these rocks include basalt, lavas (including some pillow lavas), volcanic breccias, gabbros and tuffs, crossed by intrusions of mainly dolerite dykes.

Although Drygalski Fjord's glaciers have retreated significantly in recent decades, they remain one of the most striking features of this coastline, particularly the Risting and Jenkins Glaciers. There are very few tussac areas to be found here, and the shoreline is typically rocky outcrops, steep screes and cliffs with a sparse scattering of lichens, mosses and grasses with the occasional patch of tussac, moss and burnet.

The weather of this region is windier and cooler than on the central north coast. Funnelled by the great massif of the Salvesen Range, hurricane-force winds occasionally hurtle down Drygalski Fjord, yet the same mountains may also act as an effective weather barrier, and it is not uncommon to have mirror calm waters in Larsen Harbour while 40 knots winds stream out of the fjord.

WILDLIFE

This is one of the principal breeding areas for snow petrels at South Georgia. The birds nest on the cliff buttresses and mountain ridges along the shores of Drygalski Fjord and Larsen Harbour, and mix with cape petrels on the lower ledges. During the early part of the season both species can be seen flying along the cliffs as they come and go from their nest sites prior to incubation. Blue-eyed shags, Wilson's storm-petrels and Antarctic terns are also a common sight as they feed in the plankton-rich upwellings infront of the glaciers.

Larsen Harbour is the most northerly recorded breeding site for Weddell seals. With their small smiling faces and curly whiskers, these large mottled seals are easy to distinguish from all other seals. Early each spring, about 30 females haul out on Bonner Beach and Laws Beach to pup. Little is known about the population, which is thought to be number approximately 30 breeding females. Although most have dispersed by November it is not unusual to see individuals throughout the summer.

Being rat-free, Larsen Harbour has thriving colonies of South Georgia diving petrels, Antarctic prions and Wilson's storm-petrels scattered throughout scree slopes and under boulders. It also has a small population of South Georgia pipits, commonly seen around Williams Cove where the tussac also provides suitable nesting habitat for white-chinned petrels and a colony of gentoos.

HUMAN HISTORY

On a relatively inhospitable south coast, Larsen Harbour provided a welcome anchorage for sealers and whalers. It was first charted by Brennecke, a surveyor on Wilhelm Filchner's 1911 expedition, who visited the area on board Larsen's steam yacht *Undine*. In 1922, following Shackleton's death at Grytviken, *Quest* under the command of Frank Wild, anchored in the harbour overnight after completing geological surveys in Cooper Bay. Larsen Harbour was charted in detail for the first time in 1927 during the *Discovery* Investigations and further surveys were carried out by a Norwegian expedition on board *Norvegia* in 1928. Duncan Carse's 1951–57 South Georgia Surveys prepared the most accurate map of the region, and Alec Trendall, geologist on the 1951-52 survey, was the first to fully describe the complex nature of the island's geology.

VISITING THE SITES

Larsen Harbour is the southernmost all-weather bolt-hole for yachts on this exposed coastline, and consequently is frequently visited. For experienced and well equipped climbers and hikers, there are many summits and climbing routes accessible from the anchorage. Drygalski Fjord is often either the first or final call for cruise ships as they come and go from the Antarctic Peninsula. Ships steam up towards the head of the fjord and if the weather permits, zodiac cruises of Larsen Harbour offer spectacular alpine views and the chance of seeing Weddell seals.

KING HAAKON BAY

54° 07'S 37° 17'W

Named in 1912 by Norwegian whalers after King Haakon VII of Norway.

FEATURES
▸ Historic sites of Cape Rosa and Peggotty Bluff
▸ Departure point for the Shackleton Crossing near Peggotty Bluff

POINTERS
▸ Remain on the beach at Cape Rosa
▸ Minimise vessel lights at night to prevent bird strikes

LOCATION AND MAIN FEATURES

King Haakon Bay lies between Nuñez Peninsula and Bomford Peninsula near the western end of the south coast of South Georgia. It was here that Shackleton and his five companions arrived on *James Caird* at the end of their epic sea voyage from Elephant Island. They landed first at Cape Rosa at the southern entrance to the bay, and a few days later at Peggotty Bluff towards the head of the bay. Unlike the northern shore of the bay, the southern coastline is rat-free and consequently its tussac grasslands and scree slopes are riddled with petrel burrows. Ships are encouraged to leave the bay before nightfall, not only because of the hazardous navigation but also to minimise the risk of bird strikes (see page 12).

LANDFORM AND HABITAT

King Haakon Bay is a dramatic, weather-beaten fjord lined by snow-clad mountains rising to over 1,000 m. Its coastline is fringed with wave-cut platforms and low bluffs bordered with a narrow band of tussac and backed by extensive rock outcrops and scree slopes. Following the current global trend in glacial recession, the glaciers have retreated considerably – few of the 12 tide-water glaciers recorded by Wilhelm Filchner in 1911 still reach the sea. A large glacier situated at the head of the bay descends from the Murray Snowfield into deep water. Its northern boundary adjoins a 5 km long glacier leading over to Possession Bay via Shackleton Gap. Peggotty Bluff lies on the western edge of a large glacial outwash plain covered in sparse fellfield vegetation and patterned with streams and lakes. The inner reaches of the bay are over 12 km from the open sea and thus relatively sheltered from oceanic swell. However, there is no protection from strong westerly winds that are funnelled full-force the length of the fjord and there are no sheltered anchorages for small or large vessels alike.

WILDLIFE

Elephant seals are numerous along the beaches of the northern shore of King Haakon Bay. At Peggotty Bluff small groups of king penguins may gather by the meltwater stream; a few southern giant petrels, brown skuas and kelp gulls breed in the tussac area at the bluff, and Antarctic terns nest on the outwash plain.

In contrast, the rat-free southern shore of King Haakon Bay is well-populated by burrowing petrels and South Georgia pipits. Certain tussac areas are a conspicuous dark green, reflecting the presence of dense colonies of common diving petrels, blue petrels and Antarctic prions.

HUMAN HISTORY

C. A. Larsen's *Undine* anchored for the night in King Haakon Bay in November 1911, during a survey of the western end of the island by Wilhelm Filchner's expedition. Five years later when *James Caird* made landfall at Cape Rosa after an epic sixteen-day voyage from Elephant Island, Shackleton had in his possession a blueprint of Filchner's chart. He and his

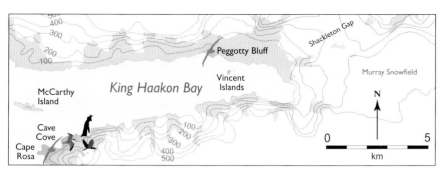

companions Worsley, Crean, Vincent, McCarthy and McNeish landed on 10th May 1916 at Cave Cove, a small opening in the cliffs at Cape Rosa. They were hungry, thirsty and exhausted and their delight in surviving the crossing was capped by the discovery of a gurgling stream of '*pure, ice-cold water*' followed by a stew that Crean cooked using four young albatross chicks (complete with Bovril). After a few days' rest, they sailed to the head of the bay and established 'Peggotty' camp near the edge of the glacier below Shackleton Gap. *James Caird* was turned upside down to form a shelter *à la* Peggotty's house in Charles Dickens' book *David Copperfield*. It was from here on 19th May, that Shackleton, Crean and Worsley set off across the island to Stromness, leaving Vincent, McNeish and McCarthy in the relative safety and comfort of the camp to await rescue.

VISITING THE SITE

The narrow entrance to Cave Cove is a spectacular, sometimes surge-filled passage for zodiacs.

Once ashore it is possible to see the shallow cave in the recess of the cliff on the east side of the beach. Landings here are limited to the beach area only, as the tussac on the steep slopes behind is honeycombed with prion, blue petrel and diving petrel burrows which easily collapse underfoot. Peggotty Bluff is more sheltered and of easier access to visitors. Although nothing remains of the camp (*James Caird* was removed when Vincent, McNeish and McCarthy were picked up by Worsley and the Norwegians onboard the whaler *Samson*) it is easy to imagine the little upturned boat nestled amongst the tussac near the bluff. A pleasant, albeit muddy walk across the outwash plain brings you to the foot of the glacier. This is the departure point for the Shackleton Crossing, a route now regularly used by mountaineering expeditions. An alternative route along the shore provides the opportunity for some beachcombing: flotsam and jetsam regularly wash up here and Shackleton reported finding a pile of timbers 2 to 3 m high, thought to be wreckage from a ship.

Top Worsley's memory map of the crossing of South Georgia
Above Cave Cove, where *James Caird* first made landfall

163

CHECKLIST OF THE FAUNA AND FLORA OF SOUTH GEORGIA

BIRDS
Breeding Birds

		ESTIMATED PAIRS (BREEDING ANNUALLY)
King Penguin	Aptenodytes patagonicus	450,000
Chinstrap Penguin	Pygoscelis antarctica	12,000
Gentoo Penguin	Pygoscelis papua	105,000
Macaroni Penguin	Eudyptes chrysolophus	<1 million
Rockhopper Penguin	Eudyptes chrysocome	very rare
Wandering Albatross	Diomedea exulans	1,550
Black-browed Albatross	Thalassarche melanophrys	75,000
Grey-headed Albatross	Thalassarche chrysostoma	48,000
Light-mantled Sooty Albatross	Phoebetria palpebrata	7,500
Southern Giant Petrel	Macronectes giganteus	5,000
Northern Giant Petrel	Macronectes halli	4,300
Cape Petrel	Daption capense	10,000
Snow Petrel	Pagodroma nivea	3,000
Antarctic Prion	Pachyptila desolata	22 million
Fairy Prion	Pachyptila turtur	1,000
Blue Petrel	Halobaena caerulea	70,000
White-chinned Petrel	Procellaria aequinoctialis	2 million
Wilson's Storm-petrel	Oceanites oceanicus	600,000
Black-Bellied Storm-petrel	Fregetta tropica	10,000
Grey-Backed Storm-petrel	Garrodia nereis	very rare
South Georgia Diving Petrel	Pelecanoides georgicus	50,000
Common Diving Petrel	Pelecanoides urinatrix exsul	3·8 million
Blue-eyed Shag	Phalacrocorax atriceps georgianus	10,300
South Georgia Pintail	Anas georgica georgica	1,000
Speckled Teal	Anas flavirostris	10
Snowy Sheathbill	Chionis alba	2,000
Brown Skua	Catharacta lonnbergi	2,000
Kelp Gull	Larus dominicanus	2,000

		ESTIMATED PAIRS (BREEDING ANNUALLY)
Antarctic Tern	*Sterna vittata georgiae*	10,000
South Georgia Pipit	*Anthus antarcticus*	3,000
Adélie Penguin	*Pygoscelis adeliae**	2

Non-breeding birds

This list includes birds reported on the island and in the waters of the South Georgia Maritime Zone which extends approximately 200 nautical miles out to sea. With increasing numbers of naturalists and birdwatchers visiting South Georgia, especially on cruise ships, many more records of birds have been reported in recent years. They include species new to the area.

			STATUS
Emperor Penguin	*Aptenodytes forsteri*	**	
Royal Penguin	*Eudyptes schlegeli*	**	
Magellanic Penguin	*Spheniscus magellanicus*	**	
Southern Royal Albatross	*Diomedea epomophora*	**	
Salvin's Albatross	*Diomedea salvini*	**	
Sooty Albatross	*Phoebetria fusca*	**	
Antarctic Fulmar	*Fulmarus glacialoides*		regular visitor
Antarctic Petrel	*Thalassoica antarctica*		regular visitor
Kerguelen Petrel	*Pterodroma brevirostris*		regular visitor
Atlantic Petrel	*Pterodroma incerta*	**	
White-headed Petrel	*Pterodroma lessonii*	**	
Great-winged Petrel	*Pterodroma macroptera*	**	
Soft-plumaged Petrel	*Pterodroma mollis*		regular visitor
Broad-billed Prion	*Pachyptila vittata*	**	
Thin-billed Prion	*Pachyptila belcheri*		regular visitor
Grey Petrel	*Procellaria cinerea*		occasional visitor
Great Shearwater	*Puffinus gravis*		regular visitor
Sooty Shearwater	*Puffinus griseus*		occasional visitor
Little Shearwater	*Puffinus assimilis*	**	
Great Egret	*Casmerodius albus*	**	
Snowy Egret	*Egretta thula*	**	
Cattle Egret	*Bulbulcus ibis*		regular visitor
Black-necked Swan	*Cygnus melanocoryphus*	*	

Chiloe Wigeon	*Anas sibilatrix*	**	
Blue-winged Teal	*A. discors*	*	
Turkey Vulture	*Cathartes aura*		regular visitor
Peregrine Falcon	*Falco peregrinus*	**	
Purple Gallinule	*Porphyrula martinica*	*	
Allen's Gallinule	*Porphyrula alleni*	*	
Solitary Sandpiper	*Tringa solitaria*	*	
Spotted Sandpiper	*Actitis macularia*	*	
Little Stint	*Calidris minuta*	*	
White-rumped Sandpiper	*Calidris fuscicollis*		regular but rare visitor
Pectoral Sandpiper	*Calidris melanotos*	**	
Baird's Sandpiper	*Calidris bairdii*	*	
Wilson's Phalarope	*Phalaropus tricolor*	*	
South Polar Skua	*Catharacta maccormicki*		rare visitor
Long-tailed Skua	*Stercorarius longicaudus*	*	
Franklin's Gull	*Larus pipixcan*	*	
Dolphin Gull	*Larus scoresbii*	**	
Arctic Tern	*Sterna paradisaea*	**	
Barn Owl	*Tyto alba*	*	
Eastern Kingbird	*Tyrannus tyrannus*	*	
Dark-faced Ground Tyrant	*Muscisaxicola macloviana*	*	
Barn swallow	*Hirundo rustica*	**	
Chilean Swallow	*Tachycineta leucopyga*	*	
Long-tailed Meadowlark	*Sturnella loyca*	*	

In 1999, the list for South Georgia stood at 84 species, including 1 introduction, now extinct (Upland Goose *Chloephaga picta*), 2 ship-assisted species (House Sparrow *Passer domesticus* and Eared Dove *Zenaida auricularia*), and 3 needing definite confirmation (White-bellied Storm-petrel *Fregetta grallaria*, Brown-headed Gull *Larus maculipennis* and Red Knot *Calidris canutus*) not listed here.

References:
The Birds of South Georgia. Prince, P.A. & Croxall, J.P. 1996. Bull. B.O.C. 116 (2).
The Breeding Birds of South Georgia. Prince, P.A. & Poncet, S. 1996.
   In Trathan, P.N., Daunt, F.H.J., Murphy, E.J. (eds) *South Georgia: An Ecological Atlas.* British Antarctic Survey.

South Georgia and the South Sandwich Islands. Poncet, S. 2005.
   In Sanders, S.M. (ed) *Important Bird Areas in the United Kingdom Overseas Territories: Priority Sites for Conservation.* RSPB. In press.
Status and distribution of wandering, black-browed and grey-headed albatrosses at South Georgia. 2005. Poncet, S., Robertson, G., Phillips, R., Lawton, K., Phalan, B., P.N. Trathan and Croxall, J.P. In press.

MAMMALS
Whales

		HABITAT	ABUNDANCE
RIGHT WHALES: BALAENIDAE			
Southern Right Whale	*Eubalaena glacialis*	Offshore(coastal)	Rare
RORQUALS: BALAENOPTERIDAE			
Blue Whale	*Balaenoptera musculus*	Offshore	Scarce
Fin Whale	*Balaenoptera physalus*	Offshore	Rare
Sei Whale	*Balaenoptera borealis*	Offshore	Scarce
Minke Whale	*Balaenoptera acutorostrata*	Offshore(coastal)	Rare
Humpback Whale	*Megaptera novaeangliae*	Offshore(coastal)	Rare
SPERM WHALES: PHYSETERIDAE			
Sperm Whale	*Physeter catodon*	Offshore	Rare
BEAKED WHALES: ZIPHIIDAE			
Arnoux's Beaked Whale	*Berardius arnuxii*	Offshore	Scarce/DD
Southern Bottlenose Whale	*Hyperoodon planifrons*	Offshore	Rare
Hector's Beaked Whale	*Mesoplodon hectori*	Offshore	Scarce/DD
Gray's Beaked Whale	*Mesoplodon grayi*	Offshore	Scarce/DD
Strap-toothed whale	*Mesoplodon layardii*	Offshore	Scarce/DD
MARINE DOLPHINS: DELPHINIDAE			
Killer Whale	*Orcinus orca*	Offshore(coastal)	Rare
Long-finned Pilot Whale	*Globicephala melas*	Offshore	Rare
Hourglass Dolphin	*Lagenorhynchus cruciger*	Offshore(coastal)	Rare
PORPOISES: PHOCOENIDAE			
Spectacled Porpoise	*Australophocaena dioptrica*	Offshore	Scarce/DD

DD = Data Deficient
Data courtesy of British Antarctic Survey.

Seals

EARED SEALS: OTARIIDAE

Antarctic Fur Seal	*Arctocephalus gazella*	> 3 million
Sub-antarctic Fur Seal	*Arctocephalus tropicalis*	Rare visitor

TRUE SEALS: PHOCIDAE

Weddell Seal	*Leptonychotes weddellii*	< 100
Southern Elephant Seal	*Mirounga leonina*	100,000
Leopard Seal	*Hydrurga leptonyx*	Visitor
Crabeater Seal	*Lobodon carcinophagus*	Rare visitor

INTRODUCED LAND MAMMALS

Norway Rat	*Rattus norvegicus*	Widespread
House Mouse	*Mus musculus*	Localised
Reindeer	*Rangifer tarandus*	3,000

Reference: *Environmental Management Plan for South Georgia.* McIntosh, E. and Walton, D.W.H. 2000. British Antarctic Survey.

FLORA
Dr. Ron Lewis-Smith

STATUS/HABITAT

Native vascular plants
FERNS AND CLUBMOSS

Hard (or small) fern	*Blechnum penna-marina*	rare, Husvik area only
Brittle bladder fern	*Cystopteris fragilis*	frequent, rock crevices
Strap fern	*Grammitis poeppigiana*	rare, rock crevices
Falklands filmy fern	*Hymenophyllum falklandicum*	frequent, shaded rock crevices
Adder's tongue	*Ophioglossum crotalophoroides*	occasional, mossy seepage areas
Shield fern	*Polystichum mohrioides*	frequent, screes and dry stony ground
Magellanic clubmoss	*Lycopodium magellanicum*	occasional, dry gravely ground

GRASSES

Magellanic fox-tail	*Alopecurus magellanicus*	locally common at Stromness Bay and Nunez Peninsula
Antarctic hairgrass	*Deschampsia antarctica*	very common at many sites around the island
Festuca	*Festuca contracta*	very common, dry grassland, especially on central north coast
Tussock grass or tussac	*Parodiochloa flabellata*	very common, all coastal areas
Alpine cat's tail	*Phleum alpinum*	occasional, various habitats, especially north coast

SEDGES AND RUSHES

Sedge	*Uncinia macrolepis*	occasional, dry grassland, but difficult to spot
Lesser rush	*Juncus inconspicuous*	occasional, moist gravely areas but difficult to spot
Greater rush	*Juncus scheuchzerioides*	common, wet areas and moss turf
Brown rush	*Rostkovia magellanica*	common, bogs and dry gravely areas

HERBS

Greater burnet	*Acaena magellanica*	common, slopes and marginal wet areas
Lesser burnet	*Acaena tenera*	frequent, dry grassland and stony slopes
Hybrid burnet	*Acaena magellanica x tenera*	frequent, with other two burnets
Antarctic starwort	*Callitriche antarctica*	common, around tussac and seal wallows
Antarctic pearlwort	*Colobanthus quitensis*	frequent, dry gravely ground
Sub-antarctic pearlwort	*Colobanthus subulatus*	frequent, coastal rock ledges and crevices
Antarctic bedstraw	*Galium antarcticum*	occasional, dry grassland and on rocky slopes
Water blinks	*Montia fontana*	occasional, seepage areas and stream margins
Antarctic buttercup	*Ranunculus biternatus*	frequent, wet areas

Naturalised vascular plants
GRASSES

Couch grass	*Agropyron repens*	rare
Velvet bent	*Agrostis canina*	rare
Common bent	*Agrostis tenuis*	common, often forming circular patches
Sweet vernal grass	*Anthoxanthum odoratum*	rare
Tufted hair-grass	*Deschampsia caespitosa*	frequent, forming large clumps
Wavy hair-grass	*Deschampsia flexuosa*	rare

Sheep's fescue	*Festuca ovina*	rare
Creeping fescue	*Festuca rubra*	occasional
Mat-grass	*Nardus stricta*	very rare, Leith only
Annual meadow-grass	*Poa annua*	very common at many sites around the island
Smooth meadow-grass	*Poa pratensis*	common
Rough meadow-grass	*Poa trivialis*	rare

SEDGES AND RUSHES

Marsh sedge	*Carex aquatilis*	one large colony, Husvik
Common sedge	*Carex nigra*	several small colonies, Husvik
Rush	*Juncus filiformis*	very rare

HERBS

Yarrow	*Achillea millefolium*	rare
Sneezewort	*Achillea ptarmica*	frequent
Lady's mantle	*Alchemilla monticola*	very rare, Husvik
Cow parsley	*Anthriscus sylvestris*	very rare
Common mouse-ear (chickweed)	*Cerastium fontanum*	common at many sites on the north coast
Diddledee	*Empetrum rubrum*	very rare, of Falklands origin
Hawkweed	*Hieraceum* sp.	very rare, Husvik
Square-stemmed St. John's-wort	*Hypericum tetrapterum*	very rare, Husvik
Creeping pratia	*Pratia repens*	very rare, of Falklands origin
Meadow buttercup	*Ranunculus acris*	rare
Creeping buttercup	*Ranunculus repens*	occasional
Common sorrel	*Rumex acetosella*	frequent at a few sites
Curled dock	*Rumex crispus*	rare
Procumbent pearlwort	*Sagina procumbens*	occasional
Dandelion	*Taraxacum officinalis*	locally common on the central north coast
White clover	*Trifolium repens*	rare
Cowberry	*Vaccinium vitis-idaea*	very rare, Husvik
Bittercress sp.	unident.	locally common, King Edward Point, recent arrival of Falkland origin
Shepherd's purse	*Capsella bursa-pastoris*	rare, King Edward Point

BIRD BREEDING CALENDAR

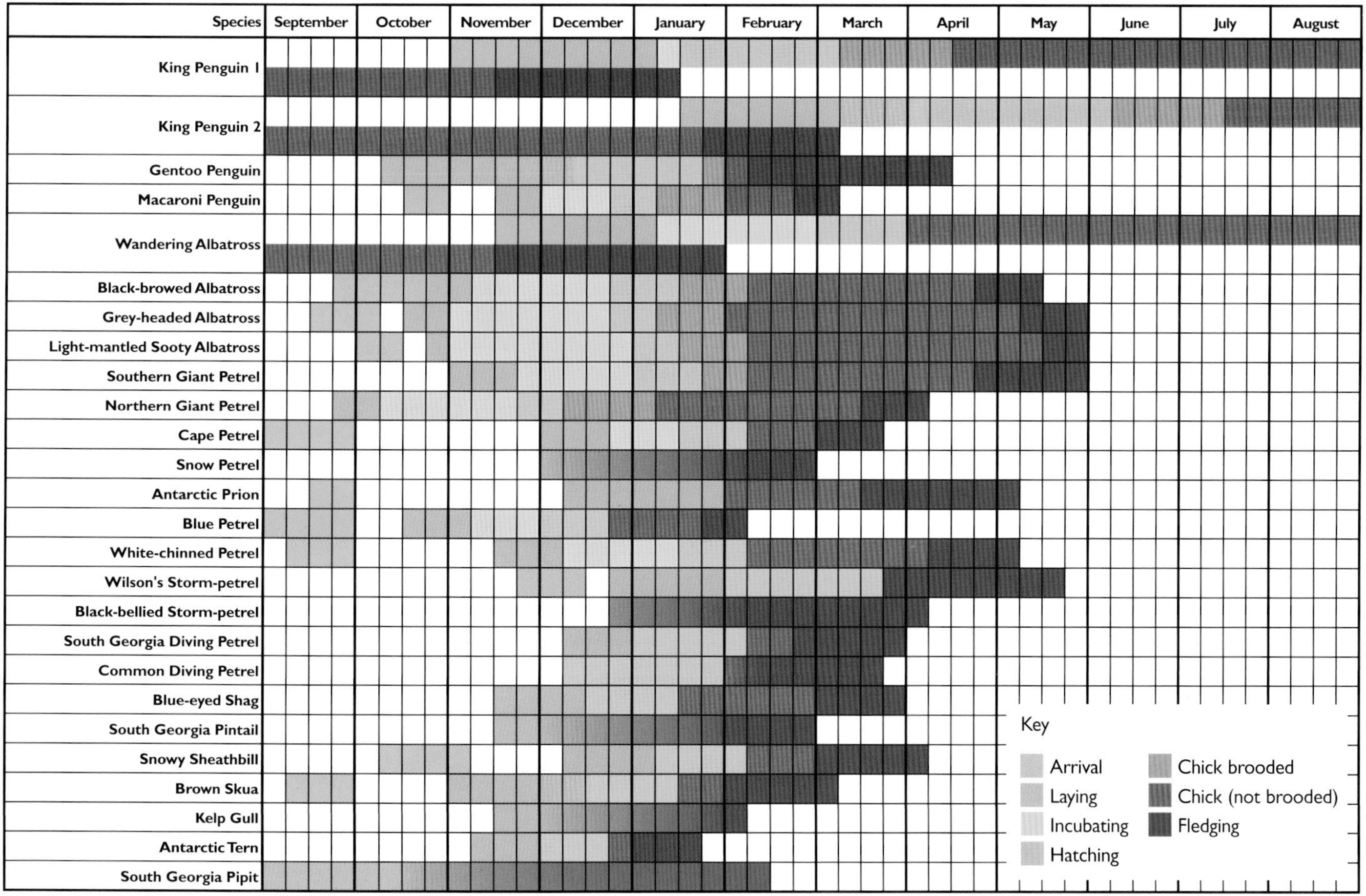

Species	September	October	November	December	January	February	March	April	May	June	July	August
King Penguin 1												
King Penguin 2												
Gentoo Penguin												
Macaroni Penguin												
Wandering Albatross												
Black-browed Albatross												
Grey-headed Albatross												
Light-mantled Sooty Albatross												
Southern Giant Petrel												
Northern Giant Petrel												
Cape Petrel												
Snow Petrel												
Antarctic Prion												
Blue Petrel												
White-chinned Petrel												
Wilson's Storm-petrel												
Black-bellied Storm-petrel												
South Georgia Diving Petrel												
Common Diving Petrel												
Blue-eyed Shag												
South Georgia Pintail												
Snowy Sheathbill												
Brown Skua												
Kelp Gull												
Antarctic Tern												
South Georgia Pipit												

Key

- Arrival
- Laying
- Incubating
- Hatching
- Chick brooded
- Chick (not brooded)
- Fledging

BIBLIOGRAPHY

GENERAL

Antarctic Encounter. Destination South Georgia. **Poncet, S**. Simon & Schuster. 1995. ISBN 0-02-774905-3.

Antarctic Oasis. **Carr, T. and P.** W.W. Norton 1998. ISBN 0-393-04605-2

Antarctide. Journal de bord d'un peintre dans les glaces **Le Corre, Y.** Editions Gallimard. 1992. ISBN 2-07-060272-9.

Damien Autour Du Monde. 55 000 milles de defis aux oceans **Janichon, G.** Transboreal. 1998. ISBN 2-9507992-8-0.

Environmental Management Plan for South Georgia. **McIntosh, E. and Walton, D.H.** British Antarctic Survey on behalf of Government of South Georgia and South Sandwich Islands. 2000.

Island at the Edge of the World. A South Georgia Odyssey. **Venables, S.** Hodder and Stoughton. 1991. ISBN 0-7515-0039-9.

Les Montagnes de l'Ocean. **Dubois, B.** Arthaud. 1980.

The Antarctic Pilot. **Anon.** R.N. Hydrographer. HMSO of London. 1974.

The Island of South Georgia. **Headland, R.K.** Cambridge University Press, Cambridge. 1984. ISBN 0521424747 (paperback), ISBN 0521252741 (hardback).

The Last Continent, Discovering Antarctica. **Stonehouse, B.** SCP Books, UK. 2000. ISBN 0-95379097-0-3.

The Totorore Voyage: An Antarctic Adventure. **Clark, G.** Century Hutchinson. 1988. Reprinted by Homelands Publications. 2000. ISBN 0-473-06431-6.

Fishing South. The History and Management of the South Georgia Fisheries. **Agnew, D.J.** The Penna Press. 2004. ISBN 0-9547948-0-X.

NATURAL HISTORY

Albatross. Biology and Conservation. **Robertson, G. and Gales, R. (editors)** Surrey Beatty & Sons. 1998. ISBN 0 949324 82 5.

Albatrosses. **Tickell, W.L.N.** Pica Press. 2000. ISBN 1-873403-94-1.

Antarctica - a guide to the wildlife. **Soper, T.** Bradt Publications, UK. ISBN 1-8983 2347-X. Globe Pequot Press, USA. 4th edition. 2004. ISBN 0-7627-0036-X.

Antarctic Environment and Resources: a geographical perspective. **Hansom, J.D.** and **Gordon, J.E.** Longman, UK. 1998. ISBN 0582081270.

Antarctic Isle. Wildlife in South Georgia. **Rankin, N.** Collins. 1951. ISBN 1-8983 2347-X.

A Visitor's Guide to the Falkland Islands. **Summer, D.** and **Falklands Conservation.** 2005. ISBN 0-9538-3715-7.

Field Guide, Wildlife of the Falklands and South Georgia. **Strange, I.J.** Harper Collins, UK. 1990. ISBN 0-00-219839-8.

Glaciers. **Gordon, J.E.** and **Baxter, C.** World Life Library. 2001.

Life in the Freezer. A Natural History of the Antarctic. **Fothergill, A.** BBC Books. 1993. ISBN 0563364319.

Reindeer on South Georgia. **Leader-Williams, N.** Cambridge University Press. 1988. ISBN 0 521 24271 1.

The Complete Guide to Antarctic Wildlife. **Shirihai, H.** Princeton University Press. 2002. ISBN 0-691-11414-5.

GEOLOGY AND GLACIOLOGY

Antarctic Environments and Resources. A Geographical Perspective. **Hansom, J.D.** and **Gordon, J.E.** Longmans, Harlow. 1998.

Glacier fluctuations in South Georgia. **Hayward, R.C.** British Antarctic Survey Bulletin, No. 52, 47-61. 1983.

Glacier fluctuations on South Georgia during the 1970s and early 1980s. **Gordon, J.E.** and **Timmis, R.J.** Antarctic Science, 4, 215-226. 1992.

Late-glacial and Holocene glacier fluctuations and environmental change on South Georgia, Southern Ocean. **Clapperton, C.M., Sugden, D.E., Birnie, J.** and **Wilson, M.J.** Quaternary Research, 31, 210-228. 1989.

South Georgia and the South Sandwich Islands. Rocky Enigmas in the South Atlantic Explained. **Stone, P. and Smellie, J.** NERC and the Government of South Georgia and the South Sandwich Islands. 2002.

South Georgia. The Rocks and Fossils. **Stone, P. and Tanner, G.** NERC and the Government of South Georgia and the South Sandwich Islands. 2004.

South Georgia - A Landscape from Rock, Ice and Sea. **Stone, P. and Walton, D.H.** NERC and the Government of South Georgia and the South Sandwich Islands. 2002.

HISTORY

Ambassador to the Penguins. A Naturalist's Year Aboard a Yankee Whaleship. **Mathews, E.** David R. Godine. 2003. ISBN 1-56792-246-5.

A Whaling Enterprise: Salvesen in the Antarctic. **Elliot, G.** Michael Russell (Publishing Ltd.), Norwich. 1998. ISBN 0 85955241 1.

An Unsung Hero. **Smith, M.** Headline Book Publishing. 2000. ISBN 0747253579.

Antarctic Housewife. **Brown, N.** Hutchinson. 1971 and 1996. ISBN 009 108510 1.

Beyond Endurance. **Barker, N.** Pen and Sword. 1997. ISBN 0850525225.

Endurance. **Lansing, A.** Phoenix. Originally 1959, reprinted 2000. ISBN 0753809877.

Glacier Island. The Official account of the British South Georgia Expedition of 1954-55. **Sutton, G.** Chatto & Windus. 1957.

Great Waters. **Hardy, A.** Collins. 1967.

Logbook for Grace: Whaling Brig Daisy 1912-13. **Murphy, R. C.** MacMillan & Co., New York. 1948.

Operation Paraquat. **Perkins, R.** Picton Publishing, UK. 1998. ISBN 0 948251 131.

Penguin. Adventures among the Birds, Beasts and Whalers of the Far South. **Harrison Matthews, L.** H. Peter Owen Ltd. 1977. ISBN 0 07206 0504 0.

Pesca. A History of the Pioneer Modern Whaling Company in the Antarctic. **Hart, I.** Aidan Ellis. 2001. ISBN 0 85628 299 5

Saga of the Discovery. **Bernacchi, L.** Rooster Books Ltd, Herts. Originally 1938, reprinted 2001. ISBN 187151022 8.

Shackleton's Boat Journey. **Worsley, F.A.** Pimlico, UK. Reprinted 1999. ISBN 0-7126-6574-9.

Shetland's Whalers Remember … **Fraser, G.** Published by the author. 2001. ISBN 0-9541564-0-4.

South Georgia – Gateway to Antarctica. **Kohl-Larsen, L.** translated by William Barr. Bluntisham Books – The Erskine Press, UK. 2003. ISBN 1852970758.

South Georgia - The British Empire's Sub-Antarctic Outpost. **Harrison Matthews, L.H.** Simpkin Marshall. 1931.

South. **Shackleton, E.** Heinemann. 1919.

The Endurance. **Alexander, C.** Bloomsbury London. 1998. ISBN 0745754123X.

The History of Place-names in the Falkland Islands Dependencies (South Georgia and the South Sandwich Islands). **Hattersley-Smith, G.** British Antarctic Survey Reports No. 101. British Antarctic Survey. 1980.

The Shore Whaling Stations at South Georgia. A Study in Antarctic Industrial Archaeology. **Basberg, B.L.** Novus Forlag. 2004. ISBN 82-7099-394-8.

Whaling Thoughts Recalled. 'A Way of Life'. **Gordon, T.** Published by the author. 2004.

BRITISH ADMIRALTY CHARTS

Chart 3596	Approaches to South Georgia
Chart 3597	South Georgia
Chart 4213	South Georgia
Chart 3585	Undine Harbour, Elsehul, Fortuna Bay, Larsen Harbour, Gold Harbour, Moltke Harbour, Right Whale Bay, Blue Whale Harbour, Cape Buller to Cape Constance, Rosita Harbour, Prince Olav Harbour and approaches
Chart 3587	Leith Harbour, Stromness and Husvik in Stromness Bay, Jason Harbour, Maiviken, King Edward Cove, Grytviken, Cobbler's Cove, Godthul
Chart 3592	Approaches to Stewart Strait, Stewart Strait and Willis Islands, Bird Sound, Bird Island and mainland South Georgia

MAPS

BAS Geomap Series, Sheet 1, 1:250 000. **Macdonald, D.I.M., Storey, B.C. and Thomson, J.W.** South Georgia geological map and supplementary text. Cambridge, British Antarctic Survey. 1987.

British Antarctic Survey BAS Miscellaneous Series Sheets BAS (Misc) 12A and 12B. British Antarctic Survey. 2004.

Falkland Islands Dependencies South Georgia, 1:200 000, D.O.S. 610. Directorate of Overseas Surveys. 1958.

USEFUL ADDRESSES and WEBSITES

The Commissioner for South Georgia and the South Sandwich Islands
The Commissioner
South Georgia and the South Sandwich Islands
Government House, Stanley
Falkland Islands, South Atlantic
via United Kingdom, FIQQ 1ZZ
Tel no: +500 27433
Fax no: +500 27434
E-mail: **gov.house@horizon.co.fk**
www.sgisland.org

The Licensing Officer SGSSI
The SGSSI Fisheries Licensing Officer
Fisheries Department, Stanley
Falkland Islands, South Atlantic
via United Kingdom, FIQQ 1ZZ
Tel no: +500 27260
Fax no: +500 27265
E-mail: **fish.fig@horizon.co.fk**

The Government Officer at King Edward Point
The Government Officer
King Edward Point, South Georgia
via United Kingdom, SIGG 1ZZ
Tel no: Inmarsat +870 382 359 033
Fax no: Inmarsat +870 382 259 034
E-mail: **sgmarine@south.nerc-bas.ac.uk**

Philatelic Bureau
South Georgia and the South Sandwich Islands
Postmaster
Post Office
Port Stanley
Falkland Islands, South Atlantic
via United Kingdom, FIQQ 1ZZ
www.falklands.gov.fk/

South Georgia Museum
The Curator, South Georgia Museum
Grytviken, South Georgia
via Falkland Islands, South Atlantic
Falkland Islands, South Atlantic
via United Kingdom, FIQQ 1ZZ
E-mail: **sgmuseum@south.nerc-bas.ac.uk**

The South Georgia Association
c/o Scott Polar Research Institute
University of Cambridge
Lensfield Road, Cambridge
United Kingdom, CB2 1ER
www.southgeorgiaassociation.org

The South Georgia Heritage Trust
23 Springfield Road, Perth
United Kingdom, DD1 4JE
www.sght.org

British Antarctic Survey – Headquarters
British Antarctic Survey
Madingley Road,
High Cross, Cambridge,
United Kingdom, CB3 OET
Tel no: +44 1223 221400
Fax no: +44 1223 362616
E-mail: **information@bas.ac.uk**
www.antarctica.ac.uk

Scott Polar Research Institute
University of Cambridge
Lensfield Road, Cambridge
United Kingdom, CB2 1ER
Tel No: +44 1223 336540
Fax No: +44 1223 336549
E-mail: **enquiries@spri.cam.ac.uk**
www.spri.cam.ac.uk

Hydrographic Society
International Headquarters, PO Box 103, Plymouth,
United Kingdom PL4 7YP
Tel No: + 44 1752 223512
Fax No: +44 1752 223512
www.hydrographicsociety.org

International Association of Antarctica Tour Operators (IAATO)
Office of the Secretariat
Executive Director
Denise Landau
PO Box 2178
Basalt, CO 81621 USA
Phone: +1 970 704 1047
Fax: +1 970 704 9660
Email: **iaato@iaato.org**
www.iaato.org

United Kingdom FCO
The Foreign and Commonwealth Office
South Georgia Desk Officer
Overseas Territories Department
King Charles Street, London
United Kingdom, SW1A 2AH
Phone: +44 2070082750
www.fco.gov.uk

The United Kingdom Overseas Territories Conservation Forum
1 Princes Avenue
Finchley, London
United Kingdom, N3 2DA
Phone: +44 2083430831
www.ukotcf.org

PHOTOGRAPHIC AND ARTWORK CREDITS

Front/back cover:
Wandering Albatrosses; Prion Island. DAVID TIPLING

Inside back cover:
King penguins; St. Andrews Bay. KIM CROSBIE
Kim Crosbie. JORN HENRIKSEN
Sally Poncet. KIM CROSBIE

3 Southern giant petrel, pencil sketch; MANDY SHEPHERD

4 Aerial view of island from the south; taken from HMS *Endurance* helicopter, December 2003. HMS *ENDURANCE* (CROWN COPYRIGHT)

5 Looking from Annenkov Island to the mainland, January 2004. GRAHAM ROBERTSON
Government personnel; Government House, Stanley. MIRANDA MCKEE

6 Around the Shag Rocks: Light-mantled Sooty Albatross. KEITH SHACKLETON

10 Gentoo penguin, Blue-eyed Shag, South Georgia Pipit; pencil sketches; MANDY SHEPHERD

11 Visitors at the Gold Harbour king penguin colony; Gold Harbour. KIM CROSBIE

12 M/S *Explorer* off King Edward Point; Cumberland Bay East. KIM CROSBIE

13 SY *Ada II* at anchor on the southcoast; Trollhul. KIM CROSBIE

14 Fields of bergy bits and brash; Near Cape Charlotte. KIM CROSBIE
Zodiac approaching macaroni king penguin colony; Cooper Bay. KIM CROSBIE
Watching king penguins; Gold Harbour. KIM CROSBIE
Visitors at the Gold Harbour king penguin colony; Gold Harbour. KIM CROSBIE

15 King penguin. KIM CROSBIE
Fur seal fur. ANDY BLACK
Moss. KIM CROSBIE

16 Altocumulus clouds; Cumberland Bay East. SARAH LURCOCK

17 Breaking wave, windspray; Gold Harbour. KIM CROSBIE

18 Trail left by marine bivalve; Royal Bay.
Fossil impression of ammonite; Annenkov Island.
Fossil impression of bivalve; Annenkov Island.
All three photographs reproduced by permission of the British Geological Survey.

THESE PHOTOGRAPHS ILLUSTRATE SPECIMENS IN THE COLLECTION OF THE BRITISH ANTARCTIC SURVEY

19 Harker and Hamberg glaciers; Moraine Fjord. PHIL STONE
Sandstone and mudstone layers; Prince Olav Harbour. GEOFF TANNER

20 Bertrab Glacier; Gold Harbour; PAUL HESLOP
Inland glacier. PAUL HESLOP

21 Glacier; Drygalski Fjord. HMS *ENDURANCE* (CROWN COPYRIGHT)
Glacial features illustration. ROB STILL

22 Moss; Annenkov Island. GRAHAM ROBERTSON
Antarctic buttercup; Husvik. KIM CROSBIE

23 Tussac. KIM CROSBIE
Fern; Larsen Harbour. KIM CROSBIE
Native burnet. KIM CROSBIE
Lowland fellfield vegetation; Shackleton Valley. KIM CROSBIE
Festuca and with tussac grasslands habitat. KIM CROSBIE

24 Fur seals at Prince Olav Harbour on beach; Prince Olav Harbour. GRAHAM ROBERTSON

25 Aerial view of Bomford Peninsula; HMS *ENDURANCE* (CROWN COPYRIGHT)

26 King, gentoo, macaroni and chinstrap penguins; Cooper Bay. KIM CROSBIE

27 Elephant and fur seals and trypots; Elsehul. KIM CROSBIE

28 Wandering albatross head. ALLAN WHITE
Black-browed albatross head. ALLAN WHITE
Grey-headed albatross head. NORMAN COBLEY
Light-mantled sooty albatross head. KIM CROSBIE
Beetle; Larsen Harbour. KIM CROSBIE

29 Reindeer; St Andrews Bay. KIM CROSBIE

30 Fly on dandelion; Husvik. KIM CROSBIE

31 Members of the South Georgia Survey expedition establishing a camp site. SCOTT POLAR RESEARCH INSTITUTE

32 Looking across Possession Bay. GRAHAM ROBERTSON

33 Early sealers. SCOTT POLAR RESEARCH INSTITUTE
20th century sealer. SCOTT POLAR RESEARCH INSTITUTE

34 Filchner's *Deutschland*. SCOTT POLAR RESEARCH INSTITUTE

35 L. Kohl-Larsen in his klepper boat; King Edward Point. SCOTT POLAR RESEARCH INSTITUTE
1882-83 map of Royal Bay. SCOTT POLAR RESEARCH INSTITUTE

36 Carl Anton Larsen. SCOTT POLAR RESEARCH INSTITUTE
Grytviken whaling station. NIGEL BONNER BY PERMISSION OF ROBERT BURTON

37 Whale catchers at Leith Harbour; SCOTT POLAR RESEARCH INSTITUTE

38 *Discovery II* crew. SCOTT POLAR RESEARCH INSTITUTE
Discovery II. SCOTT POLAR RESEARCH INSTITUTE

39 Duncan Carse. DUNCAN CARSE
Crossing a crevassed glacier. SCOTT POLAR RESEARCH INSTITUTE

40 British Antarctic Survey scientists. PHIL STONE
Royal Bay geology campsite. PHIL STONE

41 The crippled submarine *Santa Fe* at Grytviken, 1982. DAVID WELLS

42 South Georgia stamps. PHILATELIC BUREAU

ACKNOWLEDGEMENTS

Many people were involved with the creation of this book, all of whom were extremely good natured and helpful in repeatedly giving their time, comments and advice. We would like to extend our sincere thanks to all of them.

In particular, special thanks must go to the team onboard the sailing yacht *Ada II*. In addition to working hard on the 2003-04 South Georgia Albatross Survey, they were extraordinarily helpful in information gathering for this book: skipper Dion Poncet took us to all the sites while crew Ken and Edith Cripps provided succour and assistance at every turn. Graham Robertson and Andy Black willingly gum-booted across the island for the cause and they have kindly donated several photographs for the book. During that season the British Antarctic Survey teams at Bird Island and King Edward Point, the Sea Mammal Research Unit team at Husvik, and Ken Passfield, Anne Prior and Tim and Pauline Carr all kindly offered hospitality and invaluable support. Aerial photographs from HMS *Endurance* were also collected during their baseline survey and their generous assistance is acknowledged with thanks.

Onboard the tour vessels, logistics were greatly eased with the help of the officers, staff and crew of m/s *Explorer*, m/s *Explorer II*, m/s *Hanseatic*, m/s *Polar Star*, m/s *Andrea* and m/s *Professor Multanovskiy*. In particular, thanks should go to Captains Uli Demel, Paul Heslop, Thilo Natke and Peter Skog, to Expedition Leaders Bill Davis, Trip Dennis, David Fletcher, Dennis Mense, Sonja Messick, Stefan Kindberg, Anna Sutcliffe and the members of the G.O.D.S. and to Victoria Underwood-Wheatley, Baerbel Kraemer, Martin Karlson, Kenneth Keng and Andrew Prossin in the home offices.

Much of the site information and map details were collected during the course of the government funded South Georgia Environmental Baseline Survey 2000-2002, and thanks are given to the South Georgia Government for permission to use these data.

Written contributions to the book were kindly given by David Agnew, Mark Belchier, Martin Biuw, Mark Brandon, Bob Burton, Tim and Pauline Carr, John Croxall, Callan Duck, Gibbie Fraser, John Gordon, Bob Headland, Denise Landau, Ron Lewis Smith, Sarah Lurcock, Richard Phillips, Klemens Putz, Graham Robertson, Jenny Scott, John Splettstoesser, Phil Stone and David Walton. In addition Ian Thomson, Bill Romey and Andy Black also gave background material which is incorporated into the text and Katarina Salén assisted with translation from Norwegian.

At the British Antarctic Survey Adrian Fox and Peter Fretwell assisted in providing the coastal outline of the island while Peter Bucktrout, Chris Gilbert and David Walton provided images from the BAS collection. Mark Brandon, Bob Burton, Jorn Henrikson, Paul Heslop, Miranda McKee, Ben Osborne, Phil Stone,

Brian Storey, Geoff Tanner, Ian Thomson, David Tipling, Lisa Trotter, David Wells and Allan White all generously donated photographs to the book while Mandy Shepherd kindly gave her sketches. The Scott Polar Research Institute provided images from their picture library and allowed the photographing of various artefacts which appear in the book.

The financial assistance provided by the Government of South Georgia and South Sandwich Islands made the production of this book possible. Russ Jarvis, former Assistant Commissioner for the Government of South Georgia and South Sandwich Islands, provided the initial endorsement and subsequently Howard Pearce, Harriet Hall, Gordon Liddle and Richard McKee have all been extremely helpful both with contributions and constructive comments on text.

The endorsement of the book by Keith Shackleton and Ellen MacArthur is greatly appreciated with a heartfelt thanks to both.

Our sincere thanks go to Rob Still who designed and produced the book, to Sandy Crosbie who patiently proof read the text and Anya Still for scanning many photos and maps in her spare time. Thanks also to Debbie Summers for giving us the benefit of her experience in producing her Falkland Islands Site Guide Book and for helping to get the project underway initially. John Pollard and all at Sulivan Shipping, Stanley, who kindly offered printing services and computer access. Finally a huge thanks is extended to those invaluable individuals who provided mental and physical sustenance during the production: Nicola and Sandy Crosbie, Uli Demel, Harriet Gillett, Geraldine Jordan, Jeremy Poncet, Fran Prince, Jenny Scott, Penny and Rachel Still and Phil Trathan.